STONEHENGE
A CLOSER LOOK

STONEHENGE
A CLOSER LOOK

A search for the origin and purpose
of Stonehenge—its amazing correlation
with the Great Pyramid, the New Jerusalem
and the universe.

by BONNIE GAUNT

Bell Publishing Company
New York

This 1982 edition is published by Bell Publishing Company,
distributed by Crown Publishers, Inc.,
by arrangement with Bonnie Gaunt.

For more information, write to
Bonnie Gaunt, 510 Golf Avenue, Jackson, Michigan 49203

Manufactured in the United States of America

Library of Congress Cataloging in Publication Data

Gaunt, Bonnie.
  Stonehenge—a closer look

  1. Stonehenge. 2. Astronomy, Prehistoric.
3. Bible—Miscellanea. I. Title.
DA142.G35   1979   133.3   82-4311
ISBN: 0-517-383985   AACR2

h g f e d c b a

To the
Reader

—

May you discover new
and exciting vistas
as you
take this adventure with me,
for it is to you
this work is dedicated.

Foreword

When the pieces of a puzzle begin to fall into place a lovely picture emerges. The initial feeling of pleasure soon gives way to the somewhat painful question, "Why did it take so long?" The answer is quite simple. We had to wait until someone placed the right clues before us.

Thus Stonehenge has remained a mystery throughout the centuries, silently waiting for the pieces to fall together in their proper order, that its plan and purpose might be revealed. Stonehenge was built for a purpose.

Professor Gerald S. Hawkins, an astronomer at Boston University, by using the aid of computer analysis, confirmed the theory that Stonehenge was aligned to the apparent positions of the sun and moon. The computer served to lay the key pieces in order. As the picture now begins to unfold it reveals the eternal purpose for which Stonehenge was built, and the omnipotent wisdom of its architect.

It has been my purpose in this book to share with others the joy of seeing a portion of this thrilling picture. It is by no means complete. Others may yet find pieces of the puzzle which will serve to enhance the beauty of the whole.

This study has been my consuming delight for seven years. I must offer my apologies to the many friends who have found me rather one-track-minded during these years, and my deep appreciation to my husband and family who patiently endured my incessant talking about Stonehenge.

Prof. Hawkins began his book *Stonehenge Decoded* by calling the monument a "gaunt ruin." My friends have facetiously capitalized the term. Several expeditions have been made to the "Gaunt ruin" as a result of this study, and much interest has been generated in those mysterious stone circles.

I would like to express my appreciation to those who have been my help and encouragement through these seven years. First I would like to thank professor Gerald S. Hawkins for his invaluable aid in providing information regarding the sun and moon alignments.

My sincere appreciation also must be expressed to John Michell for his excellent work, *City of Revelation*. Although our independent research brought us to the awareness of similar facts, his work was a great encouragement to me, and I thank him for his contribution of some of the pieces of the puzzle.

A special thanks goes to George Tabac for suggesting that I write this book, and my sincere appreciation also goes to Robert Alexander and Carl Hagensick for their help and valuable counsel. I wish also to express my appreciation to Ruth Eldridge, David Rice, and Gilbert Rice for proofreading and editing.

Those mentioned here, who have so graciously come to my aid, do not necessarily agree with nor endorse all the concepts herein set forth.

Finally, my most heartfelt gratitude must be expressed to a loving Heavenly Father whose comfort and strength upheld me. This study has firmly strengthened my faith and drawn me closer to Him.

Bonnie Gaunt
Jackson, Michigan

Contents

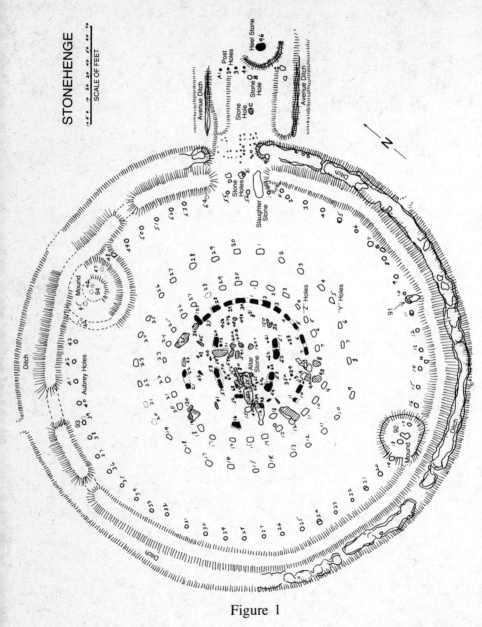

Figure 1

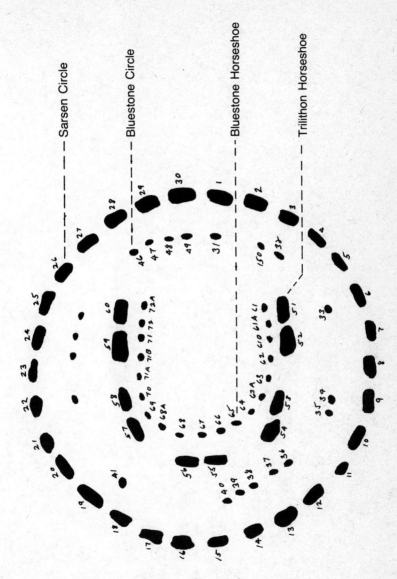

Figure 1

Introduction

Take a voyage through time and discover the secrets and forces of the universe! Our journey begins on a remote and desolate plain in southern Britain. Above us the star-strewn fields of immensity enclose us within its dome, and all around us the eloquent silence of the night falls over our awareness like an avalanche. It is the darkest hour before the dawn. Surrounding us, like foreboding sentinels from some forgotten past, loom the darkened hulks of the giant monoliths of Stonehenge. A 4,000 year old mystery still shrouds these mute stones like the mists that hang heavily over the lonely plain.

The enigma of Stonehenge has intrigued the minds of each new generation. Men have attributed to these stones religious meaning, magical powers and astronomical significance. They have worshiped here, fought here, died here. They have drawn it, photographed it, charted it; they have measured, mapped and mutilated it. They have tried to tear it down, dig it up, preserve it and destroy it. They have theorized, disputed, discovered and recorded its mysteries and legends. Men have lived and died, but Stonehenge endures!

In all the ages since its construction men have built nothing comparable to Stonehenge. Like the Great Pyramid of Giza, the solutions to the mystery that surrounds its construction, its architect and its purpose have been sincerely sought by scien-

1

tists, theologians, archaeologists and historians. Now Stonehenge begins to give up its secrets. The story that it tells not only takes us through 4,000 years of man's history, but far beyond, into the timeless forces of the universe, and into the future of man on this planet. The story of Stonehenge touches the lives of every one of us.

But why are we standing here, surrounded by these ancient stones in the misty blackness just before the dawn? We are here to watch the sunrise; and already a faint glow appears in the northeast. Today is the first day of summer. As we watch the darkness disperse into daybreak we see the first flash of the sun emerge above the distant horizon. The enchantment of sunrise once again invades our souls and exhilarates our senses! From our vantage point in the center of the monument the rising sun first appears to the left of the Heel Stone, and then seems suddenly to burst into a crown of light atop its ancient head. The ecstasy of this sublime moment fills our hearts with wonder. The mystery begins! Why is Stonehenge oriented to the rising of the summer sun?

Now that the sun has lifted the mists from the plain, we can walk about these stone circles and catch brief glimpses of the fields through stone archways that appear to be a succession of windows. For what purpose were they built? The time-worn mystery that stalks these windows has now yielded to modern technology. Through the aid of a computer, their secrets are being discovered, and the story they tell takes us on an awesome and exciting adventure through time.

Through the tireless efforts of archaeologists, engineers, surveyors, astronomers and historians, volumes of valuable data have been recorded that can now enable us to search for the real meaning of Stonehenge. But the mystery and the intrigue multiplies when we discover that the geometry of these ancient stone circles is commensurate with the geometry of the Great Pyramid in such a way that both monuments appear to have been built by the same architect.

The same architect? Fantastic! Could it be possible? Could the builder of the greatest and most magnificent wonder of the ancient world have gone to the remote island of Britain to construct these strange circles? Why? Who was he?

The search for the architect takes us on a portentous journey through time and space and opens for us a window in the sky. The intelligence that conceived Stonehenge had a phenomenal knowledge of the universe. He knew the dimensions of the sun and moon, and recorded it for all time in these venerable old stones. He understood earth's distance from the sun, the speed of its orbit and its rate of rotation, and recorded it for all generations in the circles of this marvelous monument. Stonehenge is truly a microcosm of the universe.

The search for the meaning of Stonehenge takes us on a soul-stirring voyage into antiquity's vision. The ancient prophet, Ezekiel, saw, in vision, a beautiful temple and city. Why are the measurements of Stonehenge identical to the measurements of that glorious vision?

Long years after Ezekiel, the Christian Apostle John saw in vision a city. He called it the New Jerusalem. We stand in reverent silence before the beauty of this majestic city which he saw descending from the heavens and engulfing the earth. Its outer and inner dimensions are identical to the dimensions of Stonehenge on a larger scale.

Identical? How is it possible?

Why is Stonehenge a model of the New Jerusalem? Why does its geometry become a yardstick for measuring Ezekiel's vision? What ancient wisdom was hidden in the correlation of Stonehenge and the Great Pyramid? Why are these mysterious stone circles keyed to the sun and moon and the cycles of the universe? What was the grand and immortal purpose of this magnificent structure?

Through four colorful millennia this miracle in stone has concealed its divine secrets. Can the ancient riddle truly be decoded? Come with me to Stonehenge for a closer look.

Artist's conception of Stonehenge at the time of its completion. This illustration shows more stones in the Bluestone Circle than probably actually existed.

1

What is
Stonehenge?

Standing stark and silent on the Salisbury Plain, the mute megaliths of Stonehenge endure in solemn silhouette against a background of four thousand years. They stand as a silent memorial to the intelligence, the ability, and the fortitude of its builders. It is a testimony to their knowledge of time and space, to their accurate tracking of the movements of the sun and moon, and to their intimate acquaintance with the principles and forces of the universe. It stands unique among all the stone monuments of ancient man.

What was it? What was its purpose? Who were its builders? Does it hold a message for modern man?

Historians, archaeologists, astronomers, and the just plain curious have sought for centuries to solve its mysteries. Their discoveries and observations have contributed much toward the present-day knowledge of its plan and purpose, through which those lonely stones stand mute. Yet, silent as they are, if we listen, they cry out to be heard, they beg for our attention and plead for our understanding.

Og Mandino has posed the question, "Can sand flow upward in the hour glass?"* To most men, the obvious answer is "no." But to the historian, the answer is a qualified "yes." The sands of time can indeed be reversed in the mind of the archaeologist, as he reconstructs the scenes and events of ages past. To the astronomer, the sands of time have never really moved. And to the theologian, the past becomes the guideline of the present and often a key to the future. Amidst a world of

---

*Og Mandino, *The Greatest Salesman in the World,* Bantam Books, New York, 1974.

rapid change, of incredible discoveries, and accomplishments of man that stagger the imagination, if not the mind, there stands Stonehenge. It stands in cold silence, unchanged, except for the natural law of entropy which affects all things. As we seek and find answers to its mysteries, the sand begins to flow upward in the hour glass.

The revelation of the mysteries of Stonehenge are as staggering to the mind as any of the accomplishments of modern man. Indeed, they far surpass anything of which man could conceive, for they tell us of man and his universe, and even of the Creator himself.

The means of construction alone is awesome. It is not enough that we should grapple with the "what" and the "why," but Stonehenge also compels us to ask "how." How did those stones get there?

Legend conjures up many fascinating fancies. The great Merlin, official wizard of the court of King Arthur, is said to have brought them from Ireland by the use of his "engines." The stones themselves were thought to have magical curative powers. Some of us do not possess sufficient serendipity to perceive those alleged powers. We live in a world of reality and those stones are very real. They were placed there by real people like you and me.

The visitor to Stonehenge today, however, does experience a sense of mystery, a feeling of awe and wonderment. As he walks beneath those towering, silent stones, he catches brief glimpses of the fields beyond and the horizon through windows of planned vistas. He stands surrounded, as if by walls that are not walls, by fearsome sentinels of the past; and the awesome antiquity of those timeless stones falls like an avalanche upon the awareness. It is almost as though a sixth sense were created within the mind—a sense of time and an identification with eternity.

One cannot walk amid those old stones without experiencing the overpowering awareness of the tremendous skill, knowledge and precision of its builder. To appreciate this fact more adequately let us take a look at the ground plan.

Stonehenge consists of several concentric circles, with two

inner circles spread at the ends to form U-shaped arrangements called "horseshoes." Beyond these circles, standing all alone, is a large natural monolith, the famous Heel Stone.

The inmost arrangement of stones is called the Bluestone Horseshoe. It originally consisted of 19 tall slender stones, 8 of which are still standing, 4 are fallen and 7 are missing. They are called *bluestones* because they have a slight blueish-green hue when wet. Some are spotted dolerite, others are rhyolite, and some are of volcanic ash. The latter is a soft greenish rock, none of which is above ground today.

Outside the arrangement of bluestones, and dwarfing them by their enormity, stand the stones of the Trilithon Horseshoe. The word "trilithon" is unique to Stonehenge and was coined from the words *tri,* meaning three, and *litho,* meaning stone. They are free-standing units consisting of two uprights topped by a lintel. They are of *sarsen,* a kind of natural sandstone. The Trilithons are the tallest stones in the monument and the lone remaining stone of the great central Trilithon towers above all. It weighs approximately 50 tons and is the largest pre-historic hand-worked monolith in Britain. There are five Trilithons. The uprights in each unit are so close together that it is not possible for a man to walk between them. They form a set of frames, when coupled with the corresponding arches in the Sarsen Circle, through which specific locations on the distant horizon may be viewed.

The lintels which topped the uprights were held in place by a "mortise and tenon" system. On top of each upright was tooled a knob, or tenon, which fitted securely into a corresponding hole, or mortise, on the under side of each lintel, thus holding them firmly in place. The tenon can easily be seen today on the top of the one remaining stone of the great central Trilithon, which has lost its lintel.

Both the Bluestone and Trilithon Horseshoes open to the northeast, in the direction of summer sunrise.

Surrounding the Trilithons is the Bluestone Circle. It is now composed of 20 stones which can be seen above ground. The excavations of Colonel Hawley in 1924 revealed holes where other bluestones may once have stood in the circle. In 1954 the excavations of Professor R. J. C. Atkinson, Professor S. Piggott and Dr. J. F. S. Stone revealed three stone stumps on the line of the circle. It is uncertain how many stones were originally in this circle. Some have supposed there may have been as many as 60; however, no proof has yet been unearthed to support this speculation. In the plan view (Figure 1) we show only those stones which remain today.

Immediately to the outside of the Bluestone Circle is the Sarsen Circle. It was originally composed of 30 uprights, topped by 30 lintels. Sixteen of these stones stand today. These are of sarsen, from whence it derives its name. Each of the uprights is estimated to weigh about 30 tons and the lintels about 7 tons. The inner faces of the uprights were dressed and polished. The mortise and tenon method was employed in placing the lintels, just as in the Trilithons, however, the ends of the lintels were given tongue and groove fittings. So long as the tenons held, the ends of neighboring lintels were held together so that horizontal movement of either lintel or upright is prevented. Some of the uprights were shorter than others and consequently were not buried as deeply, therefore any ten-

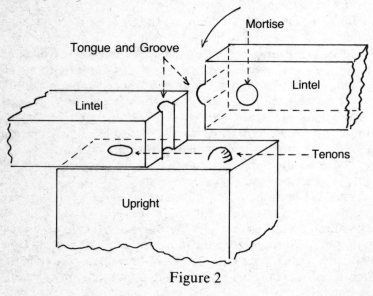

Figure 2

8

dency of a shorter upright to tilt would be prevented by the lintels which rested on it. The lintels were cut to the curve of the circle.

Outside the Sarsen Circle are the Y and Z holes. They are not visible today, having been filled in by natural processes. They were probably not intended to be complete circles, for they more closely resemble spirals. There are 29 Z holes and 30 Y holes. These holes lie on a line from the center like spokes of a wheel, each in alignment with a stone of the Sarsen Circle. Some archaeologists believe that the Z holes should number 30 rather than 29, suggesting that stone 8 of the Sarsen Circle has fallen over the place where Z hole 8 would have been. Some suggest that stone 8 fell before the Z holes were dug, and since it was in the way, hole 8 was never dug. Whatever the theory, Z hole 8 has never been found, nor has any satisfactory purpose ever been found for these holes.

Beyond the Y and Z holes lies the Aubrey Circle, consisting of 56 holes, so named for their discoverer, John Aubrey, who found them in 1666. Excavations show that they were steep-sided, flat-bottomed holes, varying from 2½ to nearly 6 feet in width and 2 to 4 feet in depth. Only 32 of these have been excavated and examined. These can be found today by concrete markers placed over them.

Standing approximately on the line of the Aubrey Circle are the four Station Stones. They formed a rectangle perpendicular to the summer sunrise. These were of the sarsen variety. Only two of the Station Stones remain today, and one of these is in a prone position.

Surrounding the Aubrey Circle is a bank and ditch. This bank is thought to have been about 6 feet high and about 20 feet wide, forming an outer barrier or wall of the monument, with a mean diameter of about 320 feet. This bank was composed of white chalk, which makes up most of the surface of the region around Stonehenge. It probably presented an impressive sight. It is supposed that this bank, as well as acting as a barrier for the enclosure, also served as a horizon for the viewing of the sun and moon through the stone archways. There was a 35-foot opening in the bank at the entrance, fac-

ing the summer sunrise. One of the unique features of Stonehenge is that this bank is within the circle of the ditch which
surrounds it. At all other circular megalithic sites in Britain the
bank is outside the ditch.

To the northeast of the circle stands the Heel Stone, a most
impressive stone of the sarsen variety, showing no signs of
tooling, but left completely in its natural state. This large un-
dressed stone is leaning toward the circle at an angle of about
30° from the perpendicular, giving the appearance of bowing
toward the monument. Some say its appearance resembles
that of the head of a fish. No one really knows how it acquired
its name, but several suggestions have been offered. Since this
stone provides the alignment of the summer solstice sunrise, it
has long been called the Sunstone. The Greek for sun is *helios,*
thus the name is thought by some to come from *helios stone.*
Others feel it comes from the Welsh word for sun, *haul* (pronounced "hayil"). Regardless of the origin, it is definitely the
sun stone, for it stands outside the entrance, marking the
northernmost extreme of the summer sun at the solstice.

Lying buried at the entrance, between Aubrey Holes 56 and
1 is the so-called Slaughter Stone. There is no evidence to justify the name. It is thought to have been an upright pillar, but
was purposely buried, possibly because it obstructed the view
of the Heel Stone. No one really knows why it was buried.
Some have supposed that this stone, along with a companion
stone, topped by a lintel, formed an arch at the entrance to the
monument. But the top of this stone has no tenon, therefore it
apparently never held a lintel. If there was a companion stone,
it has never been found; however, there is evidence that a
large stone once stood in the necessary spot.

Lying near the center of the monument is the Altar Stone.
Again, there is no evidence to justify the name. The only apparent reason for the name is its position. This stone is unique
at Stonehenge. It is of micaceous sandstone containing flecks
of mica. There is no other rock of this kind at Stonehenge.
This stone lies prone and broken. It is not known if it ever
stood upright, since a suitable hole in which it might have

stood has never been found. Its dimensions are approximately 16' x 3' x 1'9".

In the area of the entrance, somewhat north of the Heel Stone, numerous post holes have been found. Three post holes have been discovered in the adjoining car park. Other stone holes and post holes have been found near the Aubrey Circle. They probably all had a purpose in forming the necessary alignments of the structure. These are shown on the ground plan in Figure 1.

Stonehenge is built on a rather flat plain, which slopes gradually toward the northeast. Compensation is made for this sloping of the ground by the heights of the stones. Probably compensation was also made in the height of the bank, thus providing the necessary horizon for marking the alignments of the sun and moon risings and settings. It is not possible to know precisely the slope of the terrain, nor the height of the bank at the time of construction, nor can we know the exact level of the distant horizon.

There are basically three kinds of stones at Stonehenge—the sarsens, the bluestones, and the Altar Stone. The sarsens consist of silicified nodules of sandstone, sand held together by silica cement. More than 80 of these large nodules had to be found, tested for flaws and dressed with stone instruments. These stones probably came from Marlborough Downs, only 20 miles to the north, for large quantities of stones of the same kind are now found there. The sarsens average 30 tons each. Estimating that it would take 16 men to pull one ton, it seems necessary that at least 800 men would have been required to pull the stones, and still others to move the rollers and guide the sledge, etc. The task of moving 80 or more of such stones is no small accomplishment. These stones were probably cut and dressed to their shape at the place of origin, in Marlborough Downs, since there is no evidence that such work took place at Stonehenge.

The cutting and dressing of the sarsens allows interesting speculation regarding the experience of the builders. The tops of each upright were given a "tenon" or protruding knob, which fit securely into corresponding "mortise" holes in the under side of the lintels. This technique was not a method generally used in stone construction, but rather in wood construction. The lintels, as well as fitting securely on the tenons, also were given tongue and groove fittings at each end. It is obvious that such precise fitting technique had to be pre-planned at the site of preparation, for it could not have been accomplished by cut-and-fit, trial-and-error methods. One of the lintels has been found to have an extra mortise hole on its under side (lintel above stone 2). Apparently it was an error which probably was corrected before the stone was raised. Though the intelligence and skill of the builders is awesome to behold, it is somewhat comforting to know that they also made mistakes just as we do. Probably some embarrassed foreman received his lumps for that one—after all, when one cuts a big hole in a stone one cannot very easily hide it.

The method of erecting the sarsens and their lintels has intrigued Stonehenge observers for centuries. The method suggested by the archaeologist R. J. C. Atkinson is generally accepted.* A pit was first dug, having one side vertical and the other sloping. Stakes were driven into the ground on the vertical side to guide the toe of the stone down into the pit as its other end was gradually raised. The stone was brought to the hole on rollers, with its center of gravity just behind the leading roller. With levers the outer end was raised until the stone overbalanced and came to rest in a leaning position in the hole. The stone would then be raised upright by men pulling on ropes. To raise one sarsen stone would require the strength of about 200 men. When the final adjustment of position was made, the workmen quickly filled the hole and rammed it tight with stones and whatever seemed close at hand, even including some of their tools.

---

*R. J. C. Atkinson, *Stonehenge and Avebury*, Her Majesty's Stationery Office, London 1959, pages 60-63.

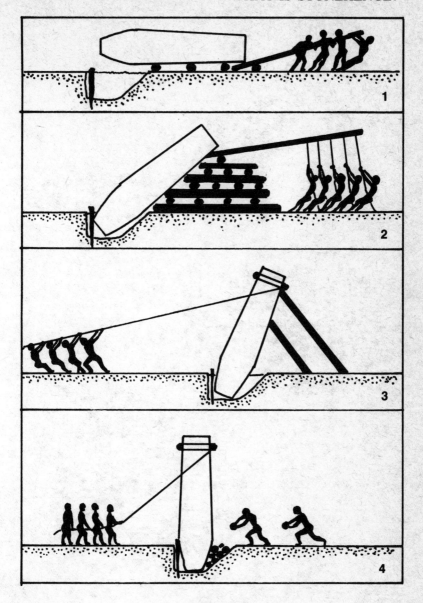

Figure 3

13

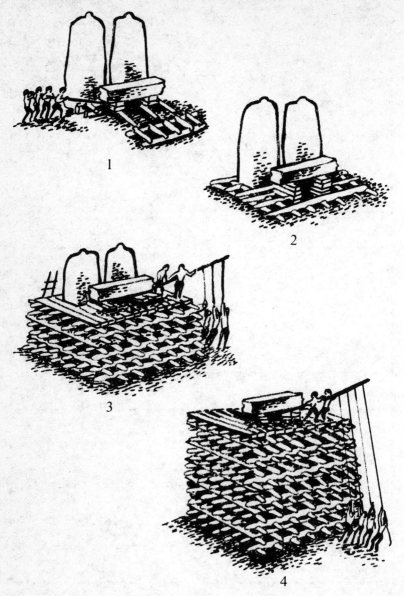

Figure 4

Raising the lintels posed a different kind of problem. They had to be lifted and placed down over the tops of the uprights. It is from the lintels that Stonehenge gets its name, which is from the French, *stanhengues,* meaning *"hanging stones."* According to Professor Atkinson, these lintels must have been raised gradually by levers and a platform made of timber. The lintel would be raised possibly a foot or two and placed on temporary supports. Then another layer of timber would be placed on the platform. Using levers, the weight of the lintel would be transferred to the platform, and this process repeated until the stone was level with the tops of the uprights. It was then carefully levered into position.

The place of origin of the bluestones was much more distant than that of the sarsens. The bluestones are found to have come from the Prescelly Mountains in southern Wales. Credit for this discovery goes to Herbert Thomas of the British Geological Survey. This required transporting them by water and over land a distance of 240 miles. The average weight of the bluestones is about 5 tons, and there may have been as many as 80 of them.

In 1954 the British Broadcasting Corporation filmed an experimental re-enactment of the transporting of the bluestones. Using a 2½ ton replica made of concrete, lashed to a simple wooden sledge which they hauled over land, the experiment proved that it would take about 80 men to haul one 5 ton stone a mile or less per day.

The experiment was then tried over water. They made three dug-out canoes, lashed them together, and loaded the concrete bluestone replica onto it. It was then poled up-stream by four schoolboys. It could easily have been maneuvered by only one. The craft drew 9 inches of water. Thus the water route through the Bristol Channel, up the Bristol Avon, was probably the one the builders chose. Then they would have had to take an overland journey to the Salisbury Avon river, up that stream to Amesbury and then overland again to Stonehenge.

The Altar Stone is the only one of its kind at Stonehenge. It did not come from Marlborough Downs, as did the sarsens, nor from the Prescelly Mountains, as did the bluestones. This unusual stone came from the Cosheston Beds of Mill Bay at Milford Haven, on the coast of southern Wales. Its transport to Stonehenge evidently followed the same route and method as that of the bluestones.

The number of men and man-hours that were required to find, transport, cut, dress and erect those massive stones is indeed staggering to the imagination. But Stonehenge is no imaginary thing. Those stones are very real and they stand today as a silent witness to the intelligence and ingenuity of ancient man.

Stonehenge, when completed, was a marvel in stone, a masterpiece of architecture; simple, subtle, stark and awesome. its beauty and design reveals the masterful genius of its architect.

History records seven classic wonders of the world: the Great Pyramid, the Hanging Gardens of Babylon, the temple of Diana at Ephesus, the statue of Zeus at Olympia, the mausoleum at Halicarnassus, the Colossus of Rhodes, and the lighthouse at Alexandria. Stonehenge, as we shall see, should rightfully take its place beside them as the eighth wonder of the world.

Yet a visitor at Stonehenge told me recently, "Approaching Stonehenge from the road by car, one gets the impression that it is nothing more than an old pile of stones that some farmer left in his field."

2

The
Chronometer

Everyone interested in Stonehenge is by now acquainted with the brilliant work of Gerald S. Hawkins in "decoding" that "old pile of stones." His discoveries have opened whole new vistas of thought. He has made the world take a second look at the intelligence and creative genius of ancient man. He has shown that our ancestors of four thousand years ago, working without sophisticated tools or instruments, created a masterpiece in stone, a monument for tracking the sun and moon, a complicated astronomical observatory, and a computer for predicting eclipses. Our ancestors were not the ignorant barbarians we have been taught to believe.

Professor Hawkins spent much time at Stonehenge observing the various sighting lines and collecting data which he took home and fed into a computer. That marvelous achievement of modern man, the computer, was necessary to unlock the secrets, to unravel the mystery, and to unveil the beauty of Stonehenge. Thanks to the luminous work of Hawkins and his "machine," the mystery is still unfolding, and those silent stones begin to speak. The message they have to tell is thrilling!

For centuries it has been known that the Heel Stone was aligned to the summer solstice sunrise. Dr. John Smith made mention of this in 1771. Such an alignment is not unique. Many structures of many civilizations have similar alignments. But Stonehenge *is* unique in many other ways.

As the visitor to those lonely stones stands in the center of the Sarsen Circle and feels the early morning mist of the pre-dawn glow, he senses a link with the past, with the ancients

17

who stood on this very spot and watched as the red ball of the sun burst forth above the Heel Stone to announce the beginning of summer. It was a moment for which they had anxiously waited. The sun had reached its northernmost extreme, and would now return from whence it had come.

Such has been the custom and tradition for centuries. Every summer people assemble in large numbers to watch the solstice sunrise. Professor Wm. Flinders Petrie, commenting on such activities in 1880 wrote, "The large numbers of people that keep up with much energy the custom of seeing the sun rise at midsummer, somewhat suggests that it is an old tradition; and hence that it has some weight, independent of the mere coincidence."

It is no "mere coincidence" that the summer sun rises over the Heel Stone. It was planned precision. As Hawkins began getting answers from the computer he realized the magnitude of that planned precision. He had not been prepared for such overwhelming evidence. He found that 12 of the significant Stonehenge alignments pointed to an extreme position of the sun, and 12 alignments pointed to an extreme position of the moon.* The more we probe the depths of the mysteries of Stonehenge the more we realize that the word "coincidence" has no place here.

After the computer provided Hawkins with the indisputable fact that Stonehenge was aligned to the sun and moon, he posed the logical, inevitable question, "why?" Why had the builders gone to all the trouble to mark the rising and setting of the sun and moon?

Perhaps the ability to track the solstices and equinoxes enabled them to plant their crops at the most advantageous time. Perhaps the sun and moon were an inseparable part of their ritual of worship. Perhaps they desired to know when to expect eclipses in order to warn the people of the impending fearful event. For the moon to disappear as they watched would surely be a traumatic experience for a people whose lives were intricately interwoven with its movements. We

---

*Gerald S. Hawkins, *Stonehenge Decoded*, Dell Publishing Co., New York, page 107.

18

could theorize on many possible reasons, but all of our conjecture falls far short of the unmistakable fact that the builders were monumentalizing, for all time, something of so great importance and value, as would compel them to carry out this Herculean task of finding, transporting, shaping and erecting those mighty 30 ton boulders. Had they merely desired to mark the seasons by sighting lines at the solstices, they could have done so with simple wooden posts. Why the stupendous undertaking, involving thousands of man-hours and many years of labor, just to enable them to record the solstices?

That they did record the extreme positions of the sun and moon is a demonstrated fact. The computer had made it irrefutable. But were they also pointing to something beyond the sun and moon? Were they pointing to time or events whose cycles were intricately interwoven with the cycles of the universe—events which would record the past, present and future? And were they led in such an undertaking by an intelligence higher than that of man?

These are profound questions, but the answers are worth pursuing, for they involve the whole history of man and touch the lives of every one of us.

In 1829 Godfrey Higgins theorized on this concept, and suggested that the arrangement of the stones represented "astronomical cycles of antiquity." Astronomical cycles, and the cycles of time and history have a relationship to one another. Can we trace history back to the time of the construction of Stonehenge and beyond in search of a possible correlation? Historians label that era "pre-history." In so doing they are overlooking the fact that the Hebrew Scriptures give an accurate record of man from the beginning of his existence.* Therefore "pre-history" is pushed back by several thousand years.

The Bible is a very reliable source of history. Its chronology is precise and accurate. But what has the Bible to do with Stonehenge? We suggest that just as the computer supplied one of the keys, so the Bible also supplies another vital key by

---

*See Appendix IV.

which we can unlock the mysteries of Stonehenge and unveil its beauty.

The chronology of the Bible is based on a cycle of 7,000 years. A *cycle* implies returning to a place from whence we started, or perhaps to the condition from whence we started. Could the 360° of the Aubrey Circle relate to this 7,000 year cycle? A circle has no beginning nor ending, and neither does eternity; but one circuit of its circumference is a finite measure of eternity. Therefore, if the Aubrey Circle were to represent a period of 7,000 years relative to man's history, it would be a simple matter to compute any given date around one complete circuit of its circumference. (Scale: 1 year = .0514285°) Surprisingly, when we tried it, we found that each of the sun and moon alignments through the trilithons intersected the Aubrey Circle at points marking important dates in recorded Biblical and secular history regarding man's relationship with his Creator. The evidence was overwhelming! Those stones had been placed in their strategic positions by someone with a knowledge of the future, for they pointed exactly to events which were not to take place for hundreds, and even thousands of years! Those events are now well-established facts of history.

Not only do the trilithon alignments point to important events, but the alignments of the Bluestones give a complete record of man's history, as we shall discuss in detail in Chapter 5.

The Aubrey Circle

As described in Chapter 1, the Aubrey Circle consists of 56 holes. These holes were placed around a circumference of approximately 905 feet, with an approximate 16-foot interval between their center points. According to Professor Hawkins these holes do not mark any specific risings or settings of the sun or moon. He suggested that the circle possibly provided a protractor for the measurement of azimuth, while the bank which surrounds it provided an artificial horizon. Thus when viewing Stonehenge as a chronometer, the Aubrey Circle becomes a "date-line": one circuit of its circumference would represent a period of 7,000 years relative to man's history. The azimuths, or the points at which each alignment of Stonehenge intersects the Aubrey Circle, become "date-points." The Aubrey Circle is like the face of a giant clock, with the various alignments as the hands. The scale for measuring these alignments is as follows:

$$360° = 7,000 \text{ years}$$
$$1° = 19.444444 \text{ years}$$
$$1' = 0.324074 \text{ years}$$
$$1'' = 0.005401 \text{ years}$$

$$1 \text{ year} = 0.0514285°$$
$$1 \text{ year} = 3.085714'$$
$$1 \text{ year} = 185.14285''$$

The Biblical cycle of 7,000 years relative to man spans a period beginning with the disobedience of Adam, in the autumn of 4127 B.C., to the autumn of 2874 A.D.

```
    4127 B.C.
 + 2874 A.D.
   7001
 -    1 (Subtract one year because there is no
          zero year between B.C. and A.D.)
   7000
```

According to Bible chronologers this span of 7,000 years is called a *day*. Biblical *days* are spoken of as consisting of *"evening and morning."*

Sunrise—Sunset

On the morning of summer solstice, the visitor at Stonehenge who stands in the center of the Sarsen Circle will see the spectacular sight of the sun rising above the peak of the Heel

21

Stone. At the solstice, the sun has reached its northernmost extreme and will now return toward the south. The intention of the builder was to mark, with precision and for all time, the exact point of the solstice sunrise.

Because of the tilt of the earth's axis a phenomenon known as the precession of the equinoxes causes the sun to appear to slip back along the ecliptic. Thus when Stonehenge was built, the sun appeared on the horizon slightly to the left (north) of its present position. Because the actual azimuth of sunrise slowly changes through the centuries, the Heel Stone was placed as a permanent marker, thereby fixing the angle at 51°51' from north.* Therefore the point at which this permanent sunrise alignment intersects the Aubrey Circle would mark 0° as well as 360°.

$$0° = 4127 \text{ B.C. autumn}$$
$$360° = 2874 \text{ A.D. autumn}$$

The visitor at Stonehenge who wishes to view the winter solstice sunset must turn from this position 178.339°.† He is now looking directly through the Great Central Trilithon—the tallest stones of the monument. As the full orb of the winter sun rests on the horizon, it stands momentarily in the slot of the Great Trilithon. Thus the builder has monumentalized, for all time, the alignment of the winter sunset at the solstice.

Sunrise and sunset mark the two turning points in a day. Thus with the Biblical *day,* evening and morning mark its two divisions. The period of sunrise to sunset ends with *evening*—and the period of sunset to sunrise ends with *morning.* (See Figure 5)

Although the winter solstice sunset is 178.339° from summer solstice sunrise, when we mark the point at which the sunset alignment intersects the Aubrey Circle, the date-point becomes 180°. The reason for this is the all-important fact of the displacement of the circles. The center of the Sarsen Circle

*Gerald S. Hawkins, *Stonehenge Decoded,* Dell Publishing Co., New York, page 173.

is displaced from the center of the Aubrey Circle by a little less than three feet. This fact has great significance: upon this displacement depends the accuracy of every date-point on the Aubrey Circle.*

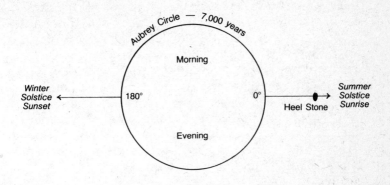

Figure 5

The point at which the winter sunset alignment intersects the Aubrey Circle marks the autumn of 627 B.C. (180° = 627 B.C. autumn) This is not only the mid-point in the 7,000 year cycle of time, but 627 B.C. marked the last year in which it would have been possible for the nation of Israel to have observed a Jubilee.

What is a Jubilee?

The law of the Jubilee, as given to the nation of Israel, is recorded in Leviticus 25:8-13. The year of Jubilee was a Sabbath of rest to the people and also to the land. It was a chief of a series of Sabbaths. They had a Sabbath day every seventh day; and once every year these Sabbath days reached a climax—a cycle of seven Sabbaths—thus marking a period of forty-nine days, followed by the fiftieth day, which today is called Pentecost. It was a day of rejoicing and thanksgiving.

*See Appendix II.

23

The Sabbath year occurred every seventh year. In it the land was allowed to rest and no crops were to be planted. After seven of these Sabbath years (49 years) a climax was reached, and the following year, the fiftieth, was a Jubilee year.

These fifty-year cycles were to begin when the Israelites entered the land of Canaan, after their forty-year wandering in the wilderness. The entrance into Canaan occurred in the autumn of 1576 B.C. when they crossed the river Arnon. This was approximately six months prior to their crossing the river Jordan. Counting fifty-year cycles from 1576 B.C. would give nineteen cycles ending in the year 626 B.C. The autumn of 627 to the autumn of 626 would be the nineteenth Jubilee year. There was not to be another opportunity for the Jewish people and their land to observe a Jubilee, for they became a vassal to Babylon in the Autumn of 607 B.C. and were no longer in possession of their land nor their kingdom.

Thus the winter solstice sunset, as it appears in the slot of the Great Central Trilithon, marks the mid-point in the 7,000 year cycle of man's history, as well as marking a very important date in the history of the nation of Israel—their last Jubilee year.

Equinox Moon

Not only are the solstices clearly marked by the placement of the stones, but also the equinox is seen to have been of equal importance to the builder. Professor Hawkins has shown that the equinox moon has been marked by a number of alignments. The equinox is the mid-point between the two extremes of the sun, when night and day become of equal length. The equinox moon is the full moon nearest the equinox.

The moon has two maxima. It does not always cross the halfway point in its north-south swingings at the celestial equator. Because of these orbit plane motions, the full moon at the equinox can be anywhere from 5.15° north to 5.15° south of declination 0°. Thus the area of its equinoctial swing is 10.30°. Because of this, several alignments of the equinox moon have been suggested by Hawkins. They are: 94-C, 93-F, 94 to Heel Stone and 94-B. (Holes C, F and B are shown in Figure 1.)

The Heel Stone is of paramount importance to the astronomical significance of Stonehenge. Using the Heel Stone for finding the azimuth of the rising of the equinox moon (Passover moon) reveals an astonishing fact. If this alignment were moved to the center of the monument (a line drawn through the center that would parallel the 94-Heel Stone alignment) it becomes the only alignment in the whole structure to pass through both the Sarsen Center and the Aubrey Center.* The apparent displacement of the Aubrey Center is thus canceled by this one alignment. But the points at which this unique alignment intersect the Aubrey Circle are startling when we consider the line of that circle as a means of measuring the history of man.

The two date-points at which this alignment intersects the Aubrey Circle are the spring of 3473 B.C. and the spring of 33 A.D. Jesus hung upon a lonely cross atop Golgotha's hill on the afternoon of April 3, 33 A.D. April 3 of that year was Israel's Passover. At 3:00 in the afternoon the Passover lambs were to be slain. At 3:00 in the afternoon the Lamb of God died on the cross. At 3:06 Greenwich Time (Stonehenge time) the moon eclipsed. An eclipse can only occur when the moon is full, and Passover is always observed when the equinox moon is full. As the moon rose over Jerusalem that awful night, it was still eclipsed for seventeen minutes.

The builder of Stonehenge has monumentalized in stone for all time, and for all to see, the importance of the death of Jesus, the date of the event, and its occurrence on the afternoon of Passover (Equinox) moonrise!

Does the other point of intersection with the Aubrey Circle have historic significance? What happened in the spring of 3473 B.C.? Yes, it has great importance, for the alignment not only points to Jesus at the age of 33½ (his age at his death), but it also points to the date when Enoch was 33½ years old (spring

---

*See Appendix II.

25

3473 B.C.). Students of Scripture often see a correlation between the life of Enoch and the life of Jesus. The first becomes
an illustration of the second.

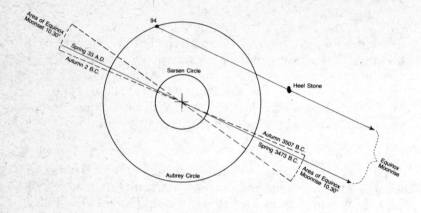

Figure 6

The builder of Stonehenge, whoever he possibly could have
been, has also shown, by those eloquent stone circles, the
place where this most important event in history would take
place. Jerusalem! The azimuth from Stonehenge to Jerusalem
is 112° from north. In other words, if we drew a great circle
around the earth which would pass through both Stonehenge
and Jerusalem, its angle would be 112° from north. The arc of
this great circle was fixed in stone. It is the alignment of Station Stone 94 to stone hole F. Neither of these stones remains
today, but sufficient evidence has proven that they stood in the
original structure. The angle formed at the intersection of this
azimuth and the Passover moonrise is 26.3026944° or
26°18′9.7″, which is the famous *Christ Angle*. (See Figure 13)
It is also the angle of all the passageways in the Great Pyramid. This will be discussed in detail in Chapter 3.

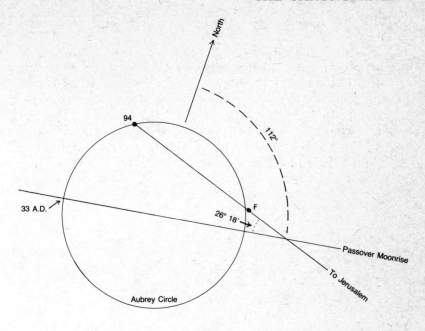

Figure 7

Equinox Sun

At Stonehenge the sun appears to move from its northern-most point at summer solstice to its southern-most point at winter solstice covering an angular distance of about 78° along the horizon. This is an average motion of more than 12° per month. It may seem strange to some that the earthling viewer, standing at Stonehenge on the Salisbury Plain in southern England, would have to look to the north to see the sun rise. In fact, if he stood further north, say in the Scottish Highlands, he would have to look in an even more northerly direction to find the summer sunrise, and further south to find the sunrise at winter solstice. This north-south swing of the sun determines the seasons of the year and the length of the day. The mean of

27

the two solstice extremes is the equinox, dividing evenly night and day.

The rising and setting of the equinox sun is marked at Stonehenge by the alignment of Station Stone 94 to Stone Hole C in the middle of the Avenue.* It traces the alignment from its first flash above the horizon on the morning of equinox to its last hurrah as it drops below the horizon at 269.13° from north. If this alignment were moved to intersect the center of the Aubrey Circle, sunset would intersect the western arc of the circle at the date-point of 135 A.D.

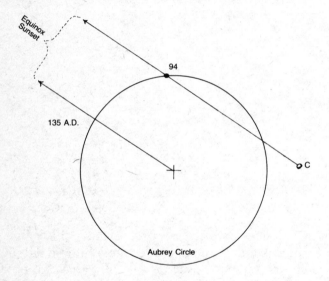

Figure 8

This date marked the end of an epoch in Jewish history. The great war that had left the Temple at Jerusalem in rubble in 70 A.D. had not entirely destroyed Jewish life in the land of Israel. Many cities had opened their gates to the Roman soldiers and were thereby saved from destruction. Jerusalem, however, which had been the spiritual and economic heart of the

---

*The location of hole C and the Avenue are shown in Figure 1.

country, had suffered greatly in the siege. The Jews refused to accept the destruction of their Temple as a final or irrevocable act. Their hopes were for the rebuilding of their sacred Temple.

When the Roman emperor Hadrian began the work of rebuilding Jerusalem in the Greek pattern, it became too much for the Jews. A new rebellion flared up. Its leader was Simon bar Kozeba. Because he was a descendant of the royal line of King David, many considered him their long-promised Messiah. His name was changed to Bar Kochba, "Son of the Star."

In the first stage of the rebellion Jerusalem was captured and once again in the hands of the Jews. Hadrian's forces quickly moved to quell the rebellion. On the 9th of Ab in 135 A.D., a war which had lasted 3½ years ended. Bar Kochba was among the dead. Jewish independence was now fully crushed.

This fateful day for a nation of Jews was indelibly inscribed in the cycles of the centuries by the setting equinox sun at Stonehenge.

Sun—Moon

Stonehenge has long been reputed to be a monument to the sun and moon. In 1793 the Rev. J. Maurice suggested, merely on mystical grounds, that it had been built as a temple to the sun. Professor Hawkins, an astronomer, found so many alignments to the extremes and means of the sun and moon that he fed the problem of probability into a computer. The answer was ten million to one that those alignments could not have been coincidence.

The more deeply we look into the mysteries of Stonehenge, the more convincing the evidence—coincidence has no place here.

photo by Thomas Gilbert

The famous Heel Stone or Sunstone. Some say its name is derived from the Greek "helios," meaning "sun."

3

Stonehenge and the Great Pyramid

"We must not let go manifest truths because we cannot answer all questions about them"—Jeremy Collier.

There is something provocative about those words!

Walk with me about those towering monoliths, standing dark and silent on the Salisbury Plain. The mists of early morning still shroud those ponderous stones which surround us like walls that are not walls, like windows with shadowy vistas, like sentinels that have no voice. It is dark, and the predawn chill seems to silence the very air about us. We stand dwarfed below those dark bulwarks, defused and muted in the morning mist. How many generations of men have stood here? How many times have they asked, "why?"

Truth! Elusive friend! Many are the truths that have been unearthed at Stonehenge. Collier was correct. Those truths which have been found should not be discarded simply because we cannot answer all the questions about them. Emerson said, "The greatest homage we can pay to truth is to use it."

We stand and watch the sun rise over those cold and lonely stones, as it has done for nearly 4,000 years, and now we can see more clearly its design. Some of the mystery fades—but much remains. That which is seen should not be sacrificed to that which is not seen.

In the original ground plan of Stonehenge, four stones called Station Stones were placed near the circle of Aubrey Holes, forming a rectangle. They have been numbered 91, 92,

93 and 94. Only numbers 91 and 93 remain today. They are of sarsen and different in size and shape from the other sarsens of the monument. Number 91 is a natural boulder about 9 feet long and lies prone, having fallen from its original standing position. Number 93 is about 4 feet long and still stands upright. It has been slightly tooled on its north and south sides. The other two, 92 and 94, are missing; however their exact locations have been charted by archaeologists.

The rectangular placement of the Station Stones was important because they served as sun-moon alignments. In 1846 Duke noted that Station Stones 92-91 parallel the Stonehenge axis, which is the solstice line. Hawkins has shown that the sun at the solstice is aligned by the short side of the rectangle, and the moon nearest the solstice is aligned with the long side. Thus the rising and setting of the sun and moon form a rectangle.

If we were to move Stonehenge a few miles north, or a few miles south, the Station Stones would have to form a parallelogram. Stonehenge is at latitude north 51.17°, and at this latitude the solstice movements of the sun and moon form a rectangle. How did the builder of Stonehenge know the only latitude in the northern hemisphere that would make its unique geometry possible?

Aside from the remarkable sun-moon alignments of the Station Stones, another fact of even greater import has been observed. The two stones which remain today are telling us something. The diagonal alignment of stone 93 to stone 91 points directly to the Great Pyramid in Egypt. The azimuth from Stonehenge to the Great Pyramid is 118° from north.* This is exactly the azimuth from 93 to 91. If this were seen as an arc of a great circle, the line of that circle would pass through the Pyramid. In other words, if you walked from Station Stone 93 to Station Stone 91 and kept walking in that exact direction, you would bump into the Pyramid. How did the builder of Stonehenge know the exact latitude where the sun and moon alignments would form a rectangle, and the di-

---

*This angle can be obtained by using a globe, or it can be computed by spherical trigonometry.

agonal of that rectangle would point directly to the Pyramid (it also being a moon alignment)? This did not happen by blind chance, as we shall see.

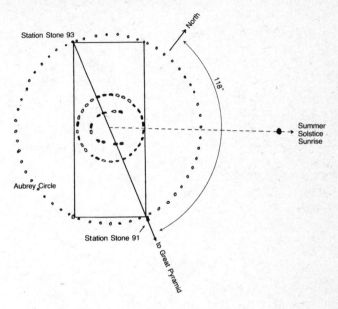

Figure 9

If these two markers point the finger at the Pyramid, then the next logical question arises: What has the Pyramid to do with Stonehenge? Is there any correlation between these two ancient monuments? Was the one known to the builder of the other? Did they, by any stretch of the imagination, share a common architect?

The Great Pyramid has attracted more attention than any other building in the world, ancient or modern. Among the Seven Wonders of the Ancient World the Great Pyramid was recognized as the greatest, and placed at the head of the list. It is the oldest and most enduring of those Wonders. In bulk the Great Pyramid is 2⅓ times the size of the Empire State Building in New York City. However, there is enough masonry in

33

the Great Pyramid to build about 30 Empire State Buildings. In fact, there is sufficient stone in the Pyramid to build a wall three feet high and one foot thick extending 5,360 miles—a distance equal to that from the Great Pyramid to the city of Halifax, Nova Scotia, Canada.

The original Pyramid was a beautiful dazzling white which could be seen from great distances because it captured and reflected the sun's rays. Those beautiful smooth white casing stones have largely been removed, and only a few remain today at its base. But enough of them remain to give us the angle from base to apex. That angle is 51.8539716° or 51°51′14.3″. This is an interesting angle. Some have called it the π angle because it gives to the vertical height the same ratio to its square base as the radius of a circle bears to its circumference. But there is something even more remarkable about this angle. It is the angle of summer solstice sunrise to north at Stonehenge.*

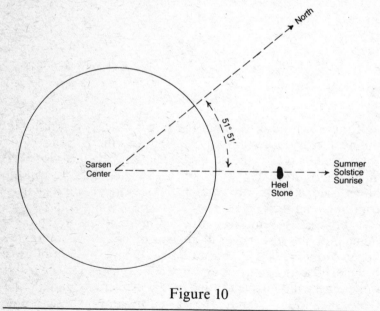

Figure 10

*See Appendix IV.

How did the builder of Stonehenge know of the Pyramid angle? Or did he? The alignment of summer solstice sunrise, as Professor Hawkins has so succinctly stated, "is not man-maneuverable" and, we might add, neither is the direction of north! Bear in mind that this angle between sunrise and north exists at Stonehenge and not at Gizeh in Egypt, yet the builder of the Great Pyramid used this angle long before Stonehenge was built.

To realize the full import of this correlation, it is first necessary to understand the time framework for the construction of these two magnificent monuments. In the early 1900s, Morton Edgar, of Glasgow, Scotland, made extensive measurements of the Great Pyramid, correlating his figures with those of Professors Wm. Flinders Petrie and C. Piazzi Smyth. Edgar found the measurements and passage system to relate many scientific and astronomical facts. He felt that the Pyramid should reveal its own date of origin by some relationship to the stars.

The noted British astronomer, Richard A. Proctor, suggested the date for the completion of the Great Pyramid to be 2140 B.C., the time at which Alpha Draconis shone down the central axis of the descending passage. Later, Professor C. Piazzi Smyth, Astronomer Royal of Scotland, agreed with this calculation, showing that on the Pyramid's meridian at midnight of the autumnal equinox, Alcyone was at a right angle to Alpha Draconis, which shone down the descending passage. Morton Edgar agreed with these deductions, and so stated in his work, *Great Pyramid Passages.*

Are there similar star-pointings at Stonehenge? Professor Hawkins, in his research into the astronomical significance of Stonehenge, found no star-pointings—it related only to the sun and moon. His suggestion for a construction date were based upon the deductions of archaeologists. Radiocarbon dating has also been used in search of the elusive date.* But the accuracy of radiocarbon dating has proven to be questionable because it has now become known that the concentration of

*Radiocarbon dating is discussed in Chapter 10.

radiocarbon in the earth's atmosphere has not been a constant, as was originally supposed.

Colin Renfrew, Professor of Archaeology at the University of Southampton, in his book *Before Civilization,* uses the tree-ring calibration of radiocarbon to determine the construction date of Stonehenge. This new concept makes carbon-14 dating fall into the area of acceptable accuracy. He found the time framework for construction to be about 2100 B.C. to 1900 B.C. This places it immediately following the completion of the Great Pyramid.

By thus bringing the dates of the origin of these two monuments into clearer focus, we come face to face with the astounding fact that the builder of the Great Pyramid knew the angle (51°51′) of summer solstice sunrise to north in the remote southern plain of the British Isles, before Stonehenge came into existence! The builder of Stonehenge could not have copied this angle from the Pyramid, since both the solstice sunrise and north were placed there by the Creator and could not be manipulated by man.

That these two monuments share a common angle can best be understood by showing it graphically. We draw them to the same scale to show their actual size-relationship to each other. Stonehenge is shown by its ground plan while the Pyramid is shown by its elevation view.

This remarkable angle is only one of the many startling similarities between Stonehenge and the Great Pyramid. It is interesting to note also that the complete circle of Stonehenge, including the ditch which surrounds it, fits precisely into the triangle of the Pyramid, just scribing the three sides. Were the dimensions of one known to the builder of the other?

33 A.D. and the Christ Angle

Morton Edgar, in his extensive Pyramid research, concluded that the passage systems had chronological significance. Taking the measurements of the passages and chambers he related them to well known Biblical dates. Research has also been done by Adam Rutherford of the In-

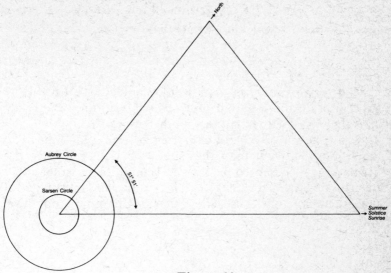

Figure 11

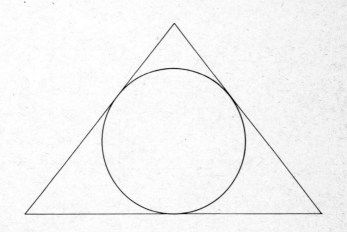

Figure 12

stitute of Pyramidology in Hertfordshire, England, resulting in similar conclusions regarding a possible chronological significance of the passageways. Both eminent authors arrived at the same remarkable conclusion—that the date of Jesus' death in April 3, 33 A.D. is monumentalized in the Great Pyramid. It becomes the great focal point upon which the remainder of their suggested chronology revolves.

That both of these authors would conclude that the same exact spot on the Pyramid represents this all-important date causes us to take a second look at their work.

Using the passages and chambers to represent times and conditions relative to man, they showed that the First Ascending Passage represented the time and condition of Israel under the Mosaic Law, which began at the Exodus and terminated at the crucifixion of Jesus. The Queen's Chamber floor level

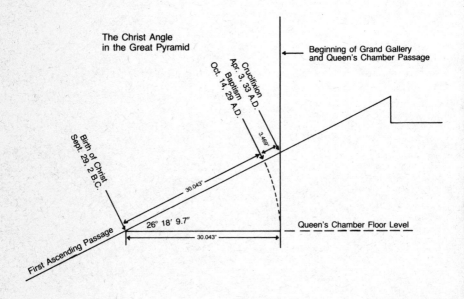

Figure 13

would represent the plane of human perfection. Since Jesus was a Jew, born under the requirements of the Mosaic Law, he would be represented in this passage. But since he was also born a perfect man he would be represented as being on the plane of human perfection. The concept that he was a perfect man is taught in the Scriptures by the Apostle Paul in Hebrews 7:26: *"who is holy, harmless, undefiled, separate from sinners."*

Measuring up the first Ascending Passage to the point where the projected floor level of the Queen's Chamber intersects, they arrived at the date of 2 B.C., the date of Jesus' birth.*
Measuring up on the passageway to the point at which the projected south wall of the Grand Gallery would intersect gives the date 33 A.D.

---

*See Appendix V for dates of Jesus' birth, baptism and death.

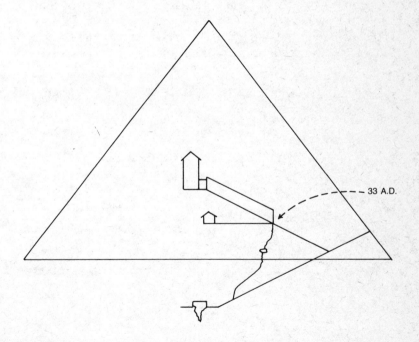

33 A.D.

Figure 14

This exact spot in that huge ancient monument becomes of immense significance when we place the Pyramid angle into the sunrise angle of Stonehenge.

With the socket level of the Great Pyramid thus lined up with the summer solstice sunrise, and the apex pointing exactly north, trace up the First Ascending Passage to the point of intersection which marks the year 33 A.D. and draw a line parallel to the socket level. This line will intersect the Aubrey Circle at exactly the date 33 A.D. This forms a 33° angle with the Passover moonrise alignment. Such a precise correspondence between these two stone structures would not likely have been by coincidence.

The architect of both monuments not only knew the angle of sunrise to north at latitude 51.17° on that remote plain in southern England but also knew the exact date of the greatest event in the history of man—the date of the death of man's Redeemer. This event was monumentalized in stone nearly 2,000 years before it happened. Whoever he was, the architect had an accurate knowledge of the future!

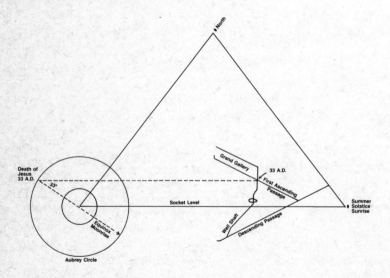

Figure 15

If any are still content to consider this mere coincidence, he has but to trace down the descending Passage in the Pyramid to the point of intersection with the bottom of the Well. From this point draw another line parallel to the socket level, and it will intersect the Aubrey Circle at 3473 B.C. (spring), the time when Enoch was 33½ years old, the intersection of the Pass-over moonrise with the Aubrey Circle.

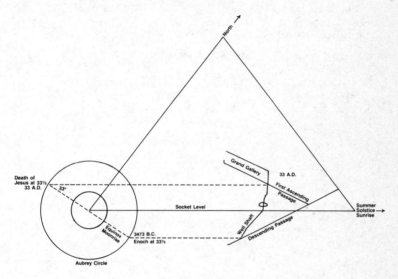

Figure 16

But why should this point in the Pyramid have any signifi-cance? Could we not have chosen any point at random which would have filled the necessary requirements for this correla-tion? No!

Both Morton Edgar and Adam Rutherford, in their brilliant work on the Great Pyramid, attribute certain prophetic sig-nificance to the passages and chambers of the monument. Mankind, having fallen from original perfection through dis-obedience to their Creator, is said to be represented as going down the Descending Passage. The First Ascending Passage is pictured as a possible way to life through the Mosaic Law. However, Jesus was the only one who was able to keep that law perfectly, therefore no one else gained life by that means. How then could man find access to the chambers above which represent life? Only by means of the Well—the way of escape. Thus the Well is pictured as the Ransom which Jesus provided, through which life was to be obtained. It is fitting, then, that the point where the Descending Passage is intersected by the Well should perfectly align with that point in Stonehenge which pictures the way of escape from man's downward course into death, *i.e.,* the Ransom.

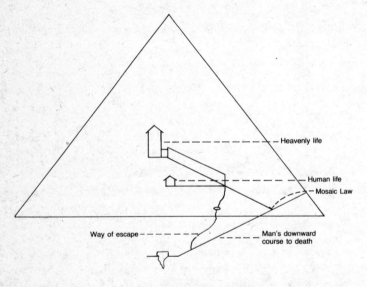

Figure 17

The Great Pyramid, Stonehenge and the Bible

If the Great Pyramid really does show the redemption of mankind, can mention of this awesome monument be found in the Bible? The Prophet Isaiah spoke of a monument in Egypt that would be a witness and identified it as the Great

Pyramid by defining its unique geometric and geographical location. The Scripture reads:

> In that day shall there be an altar to the Lord in the midst of the land of Egypt, and a pillar (Hebrew "matstse-bah" = monument) at the border thereof to the Lord. And it shall be for a sign, and for a witness unto the Lord of Hosts in the land of Egypt. (Isaiah 19:19-20)

The word translated *Egypt* is the Hebrew word *Mizraim,* which in Arabic today is *Misr.* The *Encyclopaedia Britannica* states:

> The distinguishing features of Egypt are the Nile and the desert. But for the river there would be nothing to differentiate the country from the other parts of the Sahara. The Nile, however, has transformed the land through which it passes. Piercing the desert, and at its annual overflow depositing rich sediment brought from the Abyssinian highlands, the river has created the Delta and the fertile strip in Upper Egypt. This cultivable land is Egypt proper; to it alone is applicable the ancient name— "the black land." The Misr of the Arabs is restricted to the same territory. Beyond the Nile valley east and west stretch great deserts.

From this we understand that Mizraim or Egypt was the cultivated land and that the edge of the desert was the border.

The official name of the Pyramid is *The Great Pyramid of Gizeh. Gizeh* is an Arabic word meaning *skirt, edge* or *border.* Thus the official name means, in English, *The Great Pyramid of the Border.*

Isaiah not only called this structure a *matstsebah* (monument), but he also called it an altar. There are two types of altars in the Bible, namely, altars of sacrifice and altars of witness. Altars of sacrifice were to be made of earth and unhewn stone, and no tool was to be used in erecting them. *"If thou lift up thy tool upon it thou hast polluted it."* (Exodus 20:24-25) But for building altars of witness no such instructions were given. The altar of Isaiah 19:19-20 is clearly stated to be an altar of witness: *"it shall be for a sign and for a witness unto the Lord of*

43

Hosts." Therefore it could be made of hewn stone.

Isaiah defined the exact geographical position of this altar-monument: *"In the midst of the land of Egypt"* and yet *"at the border thereof."* There is only one spot on the face of the earth that fits this description, and on that precise spot, the Great Pyramid stands. But how can it be in the *midst* and yet at the *border?* This apparently contradictory definition is true because of the unique shape of the land of Egypt.

The remarkable position of the Pyramid was first noticed in 1868 by Henry Mitchell, Chief Hydrographer of the United States Coastal Survey. He found that the regularity of the general curvature of the coast of the Nile Delta forms a quadrant. This led him to wonder what point marked the center of that quadrant. To his astonishment he found the Great Pyramid sitting on the precise spot. With this discovery he exclaimed, "That monument stands in a more important physical situation than any other building erected by man."

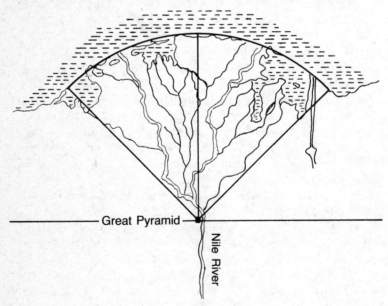

Figure 18

STONEHENGE AND THE GREAT PYRAMID

Commenting on Mitchell's discovery, Professor C. Piazzi Smyth, Astronomer Royal for Scotland, said:

Now Lower Egypt being as already described, of a sector, still more exactly than of a Delta shape, it must have its centre, not like a circle in the middle of its surface, but at one extreme corner thereof. Whereupon Mr. Mitchell has acutely remarked that the building which stands at, or just raised above, such a *sectorial* centre must be at one and the same time both at the border thereof, and yet at its *quasi*, or practically governing, middle. That is to say, just as was to be that grandly honored prophetic monument, pure and undefiled in its religious bearing, though in an idolatrous Egyptian land, alluded to by Isaiah (Chapter 19); for was it not fore-ordained by the Divine Word to be both *"an altar to the Lord in the midst of the land of Egypt, and a pillar at the border thereof"*—an apparent mechanical impossibility, yet realised in the sectorial centre condition of the Great Pyramid.

Aside from its geometrical and geographical relationship to Isaiah's prophecy, it also bears a most remarkable mathematical relationship. In the Hebrew language, the letters of the alphabet were used as arithmetical figures, hence all Hebrew writing has numeric value. Since Hebrew was the original language in which Isaiah wrote, we can find the sum of its numerical value. As shown in the table below, Isaiah 19:19-20 adds up to 5,449. The actual height of the Great Pyramid to its summit platform as the builders left it was 5,449 Pyramid inches.* All the numerical values of the Hebrew text are shown in the table below. This remarkable numerical identity of Isaiah 19:19-20 was discovered by O. de Blaere, of Antwerp, Belgium.

---

*The Pyramid inch was a unit of measure in the structural design of the Great Pyramid. It is described as 1 Pyramid inch equals 1.00106 British inches or 1 British inch equals .99894 of a Pyramid inch.

ביום	58
ההוא	17
יהיה	30
מזבח	57
ליהוה	56
בתוך	428
ארץ	291
מצרים	380
ומצבה	143
אצל	121
גבולה	46
ליהוה	56
והיה	26
לאות	437
ולעד	110
ליהוה	56
צבאות	499
בארץ	293
מצרים	380
כי	30
יצעקו	276
אל	31
יהוה	26
מפני	180
לחצים	178
וישלח	354
להם	75
מושיע	426
ורב	208
והצילם	181

Height of the Great Pyramid in Pyramid inches, to the original summit platform 5,449

The Scriptural identity of the Great Pyramid is certain, but what about Stonehenge? Is there mention of Stonehenge in the Bible? Possibly. The prophet Jeremiah mentioned *"signs"* which the Creator had placed in the earth. The Scripture reads:

> *The Great, the Mighty God, the Lord of Hosts is his name*
> *... which hast set signs and wonders in the land of Egypt,*
> *even unto this day, and in Israel, and among other men.*
> (Jeremiah 32:18-20)

Obviously the sign in Egypt is the Great Pyramid, and the sign in Israel was the beautiful Temple, but a sign (or signs) among other men was not given a location. Stonehenge could be meant. Perhaps there are other *"signs"* in other places in the earth, all of which will one day be discovered and decoded.

Pyramid Passage Angle

That the Great Pyramid and Stonehenge bear a relationship to each other is evident. And that relationship is also shown by the famous Pyramid Passage Angle. All the inclined passageways in the Pyramid slope at the steep angle of $26°18'9.7''$. To the visitor at the Pyramid who attempts to traverse these passageways, the upward climb is almost impossibly steep, and the descent through the downward passages is difficult and dangerous. Morton Edgar, in relating his experiences during his research there, expressed the difficulty with which the downward passage was traversed:

> So low is the roof of this passage (barely four feet) that we required to stoop considerably, and the difficulty of progression was increased by its slipperiness and steep downward inclincation.

Why such a steep angle? As Collier said, "We must not let go manifest truths because we cannot answer all questions about them." All the reasons are perhaps not known. But some truths are available. If we use the parallel of latitude on which the Great Pyramid stands as the base line of a right triangle, and draw a line between the Great Pyramid and Bethlehem, the angle which is formed at the Pyramid by these two lines is 26°18′9.7″ or the same as all the passageways in the monument. In case this might be considered a mere coincidence, the actual distance between the Pyramid and Bethlehem is about 233½ miles, which is the diameter of a circle whose circumference is the number of years between the erection of the Pyramid (2140 B.C.) and the birth of Jesus in Bethlehem (2 B.C.)—2138 years times 1,000 pyramid cubits.

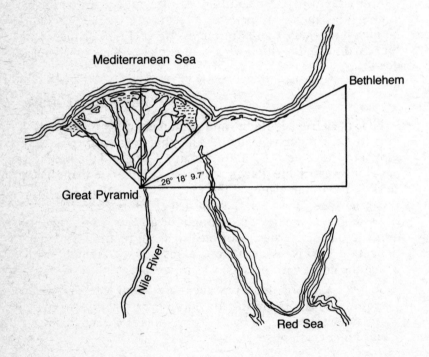

Figure 19

This most remarkable angle is also found at Stonehenge, and also points to Bethlehem as well as to Jerusalem. The azimuth between Stonehenge and Jerusalem and/or Bethlehem is 112° from north. This is also the azimuth between Station Stone 94 and stone hole F, forming an arc of a great circle which passes through Stonehenge, Jerusalem and Bethlehem.

As we noted in Chapter 2, the azimuth of the Passover moon at Stonehenge marks the date of the death of Jesus. The angle at which these two azimuths intersect is 26°18', or the Pyramid Passage Angle. (See Figure 7.)

That which is seen should not be sacrificed to that which is not seen. There are many things about the Pyramid and Stonehenge for which we have no answers, but many correspondencies have been observed. As Emerson said, "The greatest homage we can pay to truth is to use it."

Stonehenge derives its name from the French Stanhengues, *meaning "hanging stones." The Sunrise Trilithon is shown above. The uprights of this Trilithon are so close together it is not possible to walk between them.*

4

The
Trilithons

Within the Sarsen Circle stood the tallest and most impressive stones of the monument. The five gigantic Trilithons. The word "trilithon" was coined by William Stukely from the two Greek words meaning "three" and "stone." Of the five original Trilithons, only two are still intact. They are 51-52 and 53-54. Uprights 57-58 with their lintel, 158, fell outward in 1797 and were re-erected in 1958. Only one upright of each of the others is still standing. Stone 56 of the great Central Trilithon can be seen in old drawings as leaning heavily toward the inside of the monument. It has been restored to its upright setting, but is reputed to be slightly out of its original position. It is the tallest stone of the monument. With its lintel it originally stood about 26 feet, 6 inches high.

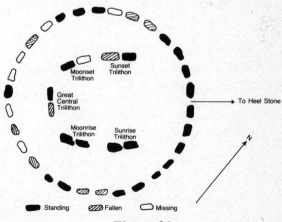

Figure 21

51

STONEHENGE...A CLOSER LOOK

The uprights of the Trilithons stood so close together that there was a minimum distance of less than a foot between them. To walk through the slot was obviously not the intent of the builder. What, then, was their purpose?

Walk with me amid those ancient stones. The slot through Trilithon 51-52 affords no view of anything, except stone 6 of the Sarsen Circle. But as we walk on, we get a fleeting view of the distant horizon as our line of vision goes unobstructed through the interval between Sarsen Arch 6-7. Unless we stop, the view of the horizon disappears as quickly as it came.

Only from specific vantage points can we view the distant horizon through the Trilithons. But as we find these positions and look through the slot, what are we looking for? All that is out there is the lonely plain. But stand there with me on the morning of winter solstice sunrise. It is the shortest day of the year. In the semi-darkness before the sun appears, we find the view through the slot of the sunrise Trilithon. It is narrow—so narrow, in fact, that the sides of the Sarsen Arch cannot be seen. Our gaze is forced upon one specific spot on the horizon. As we stand in the chill of the winter morning and feel the exhilaration and excitement of daybreak, the full orb of the sun suddenly appears in the slot.

The azimuth of winter solstice sunrise is 131.77°* from north at declination −23.9°, and when the full orb of the sun clears the horizon it appears in the slot. Its exact alignment through the slot intersects the Aubrey Circle (our date-line) at the remote date of 2593 B.C. But what significant event happened on this date that would be so momentous as to be specifically marked by the sunrise?

This is in the era that is termed pre-history. However, the Hebrew Scriptures give a clear and reliable account of a most remarkable event on that very date, *i.e,* 2593 B.C. Students of Bible chronology are aware of the fact that important events are often marked by their small and unnoticed beginnings, rather than by their high point or conclusion. The seemingly small beginning of this tremendous event was a declaration by

*All the azimuths used in this chapter are from Gerald S. Hawkins, *Beyond Stonehenge,* Harper & Row, New York, 1973.

the Creator that men had but 120 years more in which to live on the earth. This date—2593 B.C.—marked the passing of Divine Judgment upon a wicked race of men. The Biblical account from the Revised Standard Version reads:

When men began to multiply on the face of the ground, and daughters were born unto them, the sons of God saw that the daughters of men were fair; and they took to wife such of them as they chose. Then the Lord said, "My spirit shall not abide in man for ever, for he is flesh, but his days shall be a hundred and twenty years." The Nephilim were on the earth in those days, and also afterward, when the sons of God came in to the daughters of men, and they bore children to them. These were the mighty men that were of old, the men of renown. (Genesis 6:1-6)

The literally earth-shaking event which came at the end of the 120 years was the Great Deluge. The builder of Stonehenge had placed the stones of the Sunrise Trilithon in the only possible position through which the solstice sunrise alignment would point precisely to this date of Divine Judgment upon that unauthorized and contaminated race!

The Moonrise Trilithon

Walk with me a little further. The huge stones of the Moonrise Trilithon stand tall before us, and we feel dwarfed by their very mass. Whereas only one view was possible through the first Trilithon, three are possible here. Two are moonrise alignments.

The moon has a more complicated relative motion than the sun. Whereas the sun has only one extreme position in summer and in winter, the moon has two. In its 18.16-year cycle it swings from a declination of 29° to 19° and back to 29° at its north-south extremes. This is caused by the combined effects of tilt and precession of its orbit. Thus the moon extremes through the Trilithons are two for summer and two for winter.

The summer moonrise high as viewed through the slot of the Moonrise Trilithon and stones 8-9 of the Sarsen Circle is 122.746° from north. This alignment intersects the date line, the Aubrey Circle, at 2571 B.C. This is the date of the birth of Shem, a son of Noah. He is said to be the father of the Jewish and Arabic peoples (the Semetic races). Some attribute to him the overseeing of the building of the Great Pyramid. Chronologically speaking, it would not only have been likely that he was present at the building of the Pyramid, but also entirely possible for him to have been involved in the building of Stonehenge. Since we have noted in Chapter 3 the obvious correlation between these two monuments, it follows to a logical conclusion that one person may have been involved in the building of both. That this one person might have been Shem is only conjecture, but it may be a reasonable suggestion in view of this moonrise alignment which marks his date of birth.

The summer moonrise low as viewed through the slot of the Trilithon and stones 9-10 of the Sarsen Circle is 142.001° from north, and intersects the Aubrey Circle at 2251 B.C. This is the date of the birth of Terah, the father of Abraham.

The tracing of ancient chronology by means of the genealogies beginning with Adam end with Terah. From there a more complicated method of calculation must be used. The death of Terah marks an end of an era in Biblical history.

The Great Trilithon

As discussed in Chapter 2, the great Central Trilithon is in a sorry state of disrepair. Stone 56, the tallest and most impressive stone of the monument, fell in 1797 and was re-erected in 1958 by the Ministry of Public Buildings and Works. It was difficult to reset exactly, and Professor Hawkins estimates an error of about 16 inches in its repositioning. Nevertheless, the exact alignment of winter solstice sunset is 178.339° from summer solstice sunrise, regardless of the error in the resetting of the stone.

As we have shown, because of the displacement of the circles, the sunset alignment intersects the Aubrey Circle at exactly 180°, dividing it in half, resulting in the date 627 B.C. As already shown, this marked the beginning of Israel's last possible Jubilee year before being made a vassal nation to Babylon in the Autumn of 607 B.C.

The view through the Great Trilithon must have been important to the builder, for its stones are the largest of the monument. Stone 56 which has been re-erected, is the largest prehistoric hand-worked stone in Britain. It is estimated to weigh 50 tons. The Great Trilithon stood astride the Stonehenge axis and its center was 25 feet, 6 inches from the center of the monument, a distance equal to its height.

During the restoration of 1958 the workers discovered a kind of trench which lay perpendicular to the axis of the monument and became increasingly deeper as it approached the foot of Stone 56. It had apparently been dug into the chalk (which is natural to the area) and later filled in. It was apparently the ramp that had been used for erecting the upright. This stone had been erected sideways! What reasons did the builder have for erecting the largest and heaviest stone of the monument in such a dangerous and unlikely position as sideways? Perhaps we will never know. Fernand Niel, when noting this strange fact, suggested that the work was carried out under "masterful guidance." No modern engineer would attempt such an operation with the limited means available at that time.

Many researchers have suggested that a stone once stood at the winter sunset alignment on the circle of the four Station Stones. This was suggested by John Smith (1771), Richard Gough (1789), Henry Browne (1823), and Reverend Gidley (1873). In 1893 Professor J. W. Judd spoke of a small mound at that place and the evidence of a stone. He gave its position as 51° west of south. This would place it opposite the Heel Stone, and on the axis of the monument. When Stonehenge was built, sunrise could be viewed from this (supposed) stone through the Great Trilithon, across the center of the monument, through Sarsen Arch 30-1, through the slot formed by the upright Slaughter Stone and its counterpart, and across the Heel Stone. From this position, the apparent diameter of the full orb of the sun would exactly fill the slots, making it the most precise solar observatory of the ancient world.

STONEHENGE...A CLOSER LOOK

The Moonset Trilithon

The winter moonset low is viewed through the slot of the Moonset Trilithon (57-58) and stones 20-21 of the Sarsen Circle. The alignment when the moon is in the slot is 292° from north. This intersects the Aubrey Circle at the point which marks 539 A.D.

This date saw a small beginning for the papacy of Rome. It was during the reign of Justinian I that the Ostrogothic kingdom was subdued (539 A.D.) and the imperial administration was established throughout Italy, even though the kernel of the Gothic nation had not yet fully submitted. The gradual rise of the temporal power of the papacy is described in the following quotation from *The History of the Catholic Church*, H. Brueck, D.D., Vol. 1, pp. 250, 251:

> After the downfall of the Western Roman empire the political influence of the popes in Italy became of still more importance, from the fact that the popes had to take under their protection the unfortunate country, but particularly Rome and its environs, which were so often changing masters and continually exposed to the invasions of coarse and brutal conquerors. While the successors of St. Peter were so energetically interesting themselves in the welfare of the inhabitants of Italy, the latter were totally neglected by the Eastern Roman emperors who still laid claim to rule the land. Even after Justinian I had reconquered a part of Italy [A.D. 539] and converted it into a Grecian province, the lot of the inhabitants was no better; for the Byzantine emperors could only exhaust by taxation the subjects of the Exarchate of Ravenna, but in no way could they afford her the necessary protection.

> Under these circumstances it happened that the . . . emperors . . . lost all actual power, and remained only in name masters of the government, while the popes, in virtue of the needs of the moment, came practically in possession of that supremacy over the Roman domain. . . . This spontaneous result of generous exertion was in after

times acknowledged as a lawful acquisition [by Pepin and Charlemagne] . . . Pepin, as contemporary writers express it, "restored" the conquered territory to the Apostolic See. This donation or restitution of Pepin was confirmed and enlarged by his son Charlemagne, who in A.D. 774 put an end to the Lombard rule in Italy. In this legitimate way, the temporal power and sovereignty of the popes was, by divine providence, gradually established.

The event, which seemed small in its beginning, was to have a tremendous effect upon the whole ecclesiastical world. Its importance was marked at Stonehenge by the setting of the winter moon.

The winter moonset high was viewed through the Moonset Trilithon and Sarsen Arch 21-22, the azimuth being 316.560° from north. This alignment intersects the Aubrey Circle at 259.40° from summer solstice sunrise, or at the date-point of 918 A.D. Whereas the winter moonset low had marked the small beginning of papal power with civil governments, the winter moonset high marks not only the strengthening of that power, but the very saving of it from inner disaster.

In August of 918 A.D. Conrad I of Germany, on his deathbed, named Henry I (Henry the Fowler) to be his successor to the crown. Henry I was a Saxon. This event marked the beginning of the Saxon dynasty in Germany. Although Henry I refused to be anointed by the archbishop at his coronation, nevertheless his reign marked the real beginning of the church-state system which was to rule Germany for many centuries. From this beginning forward, the Saxon dynasty came to rely more and more upon the church for their practice and policy of government. At first an antagonism developed between German and Roman views of ecclesiastical law. The views and practices of the Germans were finally transferred to Rome, which resulted in the saving of the papacy from internal ruin due to the corruption of power. The Saxon dynasty became the power to nominate the pope, effecting a life-saving reform by establishing men of worthy character.

Thus the winter moonset at its low and high prophetically recorded the establishment and rise of papacy.

STONEHENGE...A CLOSER LOOK

The Sunset Trilithon

The fifth, and last of the gigantic Trilithons is the Sunset Trilithon (59-60). Upright 60 once had a deep natural cavity near the bottom of its outer face, but because it was felt the stone might break, the cavity has been filled with concrete. Upright 59 lies prone beside it, broken into three pieces. The lintel which topped them has also been broken; one piece was thrown more than 25 feet away from the Trilithon.

As it stood originally, the slot through the Sunset Trilithon and Sarsen Arch 23-24 provided the alignment of the summer solstice sunset. The azimuth of the alignment is 307.267° from north at a declination of +23.906°. This is 261.647° from summer solstice sunrise on the Aubrey Circle, giving the date-point of spring 962 A.D.

On February 2, 962 A.D., Otto the Great, son of Henry the Fowler, was crowned emperor of the Holy Roman Empire. For the eleven years of his reign he brought stability to the Empire. His object was not to make the state religious but the church political. The clergy must first be officials of the king, and secondly members of an ecclesiastical order. The relation of the Empire to the papacy dominated the history of Europe for the next three centuries following his coronation. The relation was one of amity. The pope and the emperor stood as co-ordinate sovereigns, ruling together the commonwealth of Europe. The Holy Roman Empire rose to its zenith.

Three-stones

Trilithon is a word coined from the two Greek words meaning "three" and "stone." It is unique at Stonehenge. But why three stones? The obvious answer would be that three stones are required to make an arch. However, there may be a deeper and more meaningful explanation.

The number *three* as used in the Bible has a special significance, as do many Biblical numbers. Three is used to denote a transition from one era to another. For example: Jesus was in the grave for parts of three days—the end of an era for man-

58

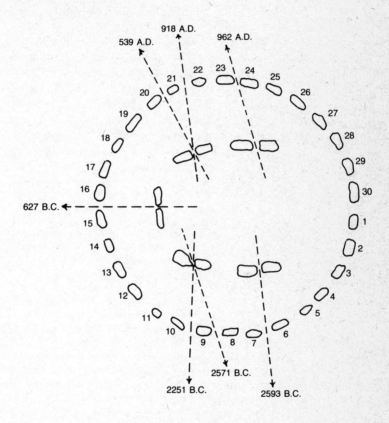

Figure 22

59

kind and the beginning of a new era. Or, again, take the example of Moses receiving the Law of God on Mount Sinai. It was given on the third day (Exodus 19 & 20). This marked the end of an era and the beginning of a new one in which the nation of Israel was under covenant relationship to their God.

So at Stonehenge, the number three follows the same rule. The Trilithons, three-stones, each mark the ending of an era and the beginning of a new. As we saw, the Sunrise Trilithon marked the date when Divine Judgment was pronounced upon an unauthorized and wicked race, bringing to an end that era in the Great Deluge catastrophe, and ushering in a new era under righteous Noah and his family. The Moonrise Trilithon marked the end of an era and ushered in a new one in which a man called Abraham became the father of a nation. The Great Trilithon marked the date which began the end of an era for the nation of Israel which resulted in their captivity and bondage to Babylon. And the Moonset and Sunset Trilithons mark the end of an era and the beginning and development to its zenith of the papacy and the church-state form of government by the Holy Roman Empire.

As we walk about those towering stones of the Trilithons, the view through the slot gives us a look at the distant horizon, and at the precise risings and settings of the sun and moon. But these are merely the physical evidences of something far greater. Looking beyond, we begin to get an insight into history written in advance, monumentalized in stone.

5

The Bluestones

"Time, whose tooth gnaws away everything else, is powerless against truth."—Thomas Huxley

What is time? This universal physician, this revealer of all that is hidden, this friend and foe of man—time—is the measure by which we record the passing of events. Time is not only *"powerless against truth,"* it lays truth bare for all to see. Or, to put it in the words of Euripides: "Time will discover everything to posterity; it is a babbler, and speaks even when no question is put." But anyone who beholds those lonely, timeless stones on Salisbury Plain will put the question—"Why?"

Like the rains that wildly sweep across that lonely plain, time relentlessly drifts across those silent stones, but time is powerless against the truth they hold within. Stonehenge, like a giant clock, ticks away the days, the years, the ages, and leaves for us the silent record set in stone. The bluestones tell the history of man. The bluestones tell the time.

What are the bluestones? There are two arrangements of bluestones. One just inside the Sarsen Circle is called the Bluestone Circle. The other, just inside the trilithons, is called the Bluestone Horseshoe, for it is an open-ended circle. These monoliths are smaller than the sarsen stones and belong to a different geological formation. They are of the same composition as granite—eruptive rocks—known in geology as dolerite and rhyolite. The name bluestones comes from their blueish tint when wet. Of the twenty stones remaining in the Bluestone Circle, sixteen are dolerite and four are rhyolite. The bluestones of the circle are untooled monoliths, while

61

those of the horseshoe have been given a conical shape, like an obelisk. A few of them are flat on the top.

Archaeologists and authors are in wide disagreement on the number of bluestones in the original circle. Petrie believed that the Bluestone Circle was never finished. Stukely, in 1723, suggested that there were forty stones in the circle. In 1956 archaeologists Piggott and Atkinson found fragments of bluestones and holes that probably held stones, and suggested that the number may have been considerably more, perhaps sixty. Today only six are still standing, five are leaning, seven are lying on the ground, and some are merely small stumps.

An interesting observation was made by Robert Newall. He pointed out that the bluestones which remain in the circle today are directly opposite one another in relation to the center, *i.e.,* they are arranged in pairs at opposite ends of a single diameter. This led him to suggest that perhaps the original number of stones in the circle was not much greater than the number remaining today, for if some stones had been taken away, it is highly unlikely that vandals would have removed them in pairs.

Herbert Thomas, of the British Geological Survey, discovered that the bluestones came from the Prescelly Mountains in southern Wales—a distance, as the crow flies, of about 135 miles. But since the builder did not have Merlin's magic "machines," those monoliths had to be transported terrestrially. The distance by water and over land was probably about 240 miles. Since the average weight was about five tons each, it meant no small feat to quarry and transport them. Hawkins calculated it would have taken 209,290 man-days just to transport them from the Prescelly Mountains to Salisbury Plain.

The builder of Stonehenge displayed his knowledge of geometry by the placing of the circles and horseshoes. The ratio between the areas of the Sarsen and Bluestone Circles (the ratio between the squares of their radii) is 1.6 to 1. This shows that the builder not only understood the function of π (pi) and could calculate the area of a circle, but additionally he understood the function of φ (phi), the Golden Section, which gives the monument its pleasing sense of balance and proportion.

The inner faces of the stones in the Bluestone Circle which are standing today are tangent to a circle whose diameter is about 76 feet. Atkinson gives 75 feet and E. H. Stone gives 76½ feet. Therefore, allowing for the thickness of the stones, their outer diameter has been estimated originally to have been about 79 feet. This gives a circumference of approximately 248 feet or roughly 144 royal cubits.

If the circumference of the Sarsen Circle (316.8 feet)* were taken as the perimeter of a square, a circle inscribed within that square would have a diameter of 79.2 feet and a circumference of 144 royal cubits.

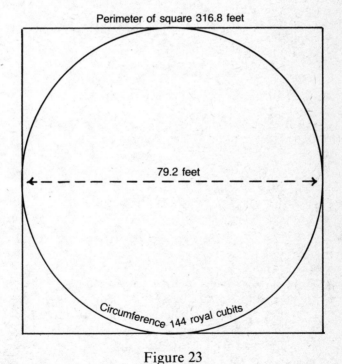

Figure 23

*See Chapter 7, The Amazing Sarsen Circle, for a more complete definition of its circumference.

Now inscribe an equilateral triangle within the Bluestone Circle and inscribe a circle within the triangle. The diameter of that circle will be 39.6 feet, which is the diameter of the circle upon which the Bluestone Horseshoe is built. Surely the builder had a knowledge of geometry and the ability to apply it to architectural design.

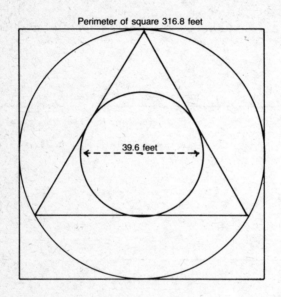

Figure 24

For purposes of identification, all the stones of the monument have been given numbers. This numbering system was first used by Petrie, and has been unanimously adopted by all British authors. In the Sarsen Circle missing stones have been given numbers, however in the Bluestone Circle and Horseshoe they have not. We show missing stones in the Horseshoe by the number of the stone which precedes it, followed by A, B, etc. In the Bluestone Circle only existing stones are shown.

The Bluestone Clock

When considering the chronological function of the monument, a line drawn from the Sarsen Center across the center of a bluestone will intersect the Aubrey Circle (the date-line) at a significant date-point in man's history. The bluestones, like a giant clock, tell the history of man.

We will begin with the first bluestone on the right of the axis of symmetry and proceed around the circle, taking each one in its natural chronological order, whether it be in the circle or in the horseshoe, and show the importance of the events which are marked by the respective date-points. The amazing accuracy of the bluestones cries aloud that the builder was one who had a knowledge of history before the fact.

A few feet to the right of the axis stands stone 31. It is of dolerite. If we draw a line from the Sarsen Center across the center of this stone, it will intersect the Aubrey Circle at 6.582° from summer solstice sunrise, which gives it a date-point of 3999 B.C. We are in the area of pre-history. But again, the Hebrew Scriptures provide an accurate record of time and events. This remote date of 3999 B.C. is the year of the birth of Seth.

Seth was the third son of Adam who received mention in Scripture. There were undoubtedly many other sons and daughters born to Adam and Eve, but only three are mentioned by name because these three played an important role in the history of man. The firstborn was Cain; the second was Abel (possibly the twin of Cain but born second). When these two sons matured, Cain developed a jealousy toward Abel which led him to commit murder. Thus another son, Seth, was given to Adam and Eve to take the place of Abel.

And Adam knew his wife again; and she bare a son, and called his name Seth: for God, said she, hath appointed me another seed instead of Abel, whom Cain slew. (Genesis 4:25)

The birth of Seth is important to the history of man, for it was through his line of descent that Jesus was born.

The next stone to the right in the circle is 150. All the stones of the circle and horseshoe have been given two-digit numbers except this one. At present it lies prone beneath the half fallen stone 32. All the lintels of the monument have been given three-digit numbers. When Petrie devised the system of numbering, he noticed that this stone had two mortise holes in one of its sides, thus he gave it a lintel number. Many theories have been suggested regarding the purpose of the mortises, some suggesting that it was once part of a bluestone trilithon. Controversy has raged over that hypothetical trilithon, but most authors reject it. The fact remains that this bluestone lies in the Bluestone Circle and it has two mortises. What archaeologists make of it is purely conjectural. No suggestions are attempted here.

It is difficult to drawn an accurate alignment from the center across this stone for it is lying prone and out of its original position. Some ground plans show the stone where it probably stood originally. A line drawn from the center across this stone would intersect the Aubrey Circle at the approximate date-point of 3611 ± B.C. No significant event can be found which would give this date importance.

Passing to the next stone in the circle, 32, which is half lying on 150, we find it is also of dolerite. The position of this stone is of much interest. Using the alignment across its center as near as can be determined from the ground plans available, it will intersect the Aubrey Circle at the date-point of 3473 B.C. As has been shown in Chapter 2, this was the date when Enoch was 33½ years old. Enoch at 33½ was an illustration of Jesus at 33½. The alignment from the center across stone 32 lies on the azimuth of equinox moonrise (Passover moonrise) which intersects the other side of the Aubrey Circle at 33 A.D. (spring), when Jesus was 33½ years old. Jesus died on the afternoon of Passover moonrise, April 3, 33 A.D.

This stone, 32, corresponds exactly with bluestone 41. They lie at opposite ends of a single diameter which passes through the Sarsen Center. This alignment lies on the azimuth of Passover moonrise, and points to the west to Jesus at 33½, and to the east to Enoch at 33½.

Taking the bluestones in the order of their chronological significance, we move to the first stone of the horseshoe, number 61. If we draw a line from the center across this stone it intersects the Aubrey Circle at the date-point of 3199 B.C., the date of the death of Adam.

In Genesis 2:17 a law was given to Adam, as well as the penalty for the breaking of it. *"But of the tree of the knowledge of good and evil, thou shalt not eat of it; for in the day that thou eatest thereof, dying thou shalt die."* But Adam lived to be 930 years old. The Hebrew Scriptures use the word *day* to denote a specific period of time. It was the Apostle Peter who gave us the definition of the length of a *day* in the ante-diluvian world: *"The world that then was, being overflowed with water, perished . . . Be not ignorant of this one thing, that one day is with the Lord as a thousand years . . ."* (II Peter 3:6-8)

The life span of ante-diluvian man was much greater than it is today for two important reasons, both of which had to do with the vapor canopy which fell in 2473 B.C. during the Great Deluge. As long as the vapor canopy surrounded our planet, it filtered out the ultra-violet rays of the sun which are harmful to man. Also, the formation of ozone (O_3), which is caused by the action of the ultra-violet rays upon the oxygen atoms (O_2) could not occur beneath the vapor canopy. Ozone is a deadly poison to man. The formation of an ozone layer above the canopy further served to filter the ultra-violet rays from reaching man. When the vapor canopy fell in the form of rain at the time of the Great Deluge, the ozone layer remained, thereby continuing to shield man somewhat, but to a lesser degree, from the harmful effects of ultra-violet radiation. Today there is much concern among scientists and environmentalists regarding the harmful effects of fluorocarbons upon the ozone layer. If this layer were destroyed, or even impaired, it would shorten the life span of man and could have a serious effect upon the human race.

Immediately following the Great Deluge the life span of man was cut almost precisely in half.

Adam's life span of 930 years was normal for the ante-diluvian era. But, as his Creator had decreed, he was to die within a *day*—within a thousand years. No man has lived beyond the length of Adam's *day*. Methuselah lived the longest of any man recorded in history. According to the Hebrew Scriptures he lived to be 969 years old, dying in the same year as the flood catastrophe.

Thus stone 61 of the Bluestone Horseshoe provides the alignment which marks the carrying out of the sentence placed upon Adam—*"In the day that thou eatest thereof, dying thou shalt die."* Before that thousand year day came to a close, Adam died. The year was 3199 B.C.

Several stones of the horseshoe are missing, but have been shown, without identifying numbers, on some ground plans. These plans show a stone next to 61 equally spaced with the other stones of the horseshoe. We will designate it 61A. If indeed a stone once stood in this spot its alignment from the center would intersect the Aubrey Circle at the date-point 3073 B.C., the year of the birth of Noah.

Noah was an important figure in the history of man, for he was the one used by the Creator to save a nucleus of the human race at the time of the flood catastrophe.

The next stone in the chronological order of the bluestones is number 33 of the circle. Its alignment from the center intersects the Aubrey Circle at about 2843 ± B.C. This would be sometime during the life of Noah, but prior to the Great Deluge. No significant event can be found to mark this date, however the alignment is of interest because of its azimuth from north. It is 118° from north, which is the azimuth from Stonehenge to the Great Pyramid. Thus this alignment becomes the arc of a great circle, the line of which would pass through both Stonehenge and the Pyramid.

Next in order is a missing stone of the horseshoe, which we will designate 61B. Since it appears on some ground plans it is included here. No significant date, however, can be found from its alignment with center. A line drawn from the center across this stone would intersect the Aubrey Circle at 2804 ± B.C. This is still during the life of Noah prior to the Deluge.

To the right of this stands stone 62 of the horseshoe. It stands upright in its original position and, like all the stones of the horseshoe, it is of dolerite. A line drawn from the Sarsen Center across this stone intersects the Aubrey Circle at the famous date-point 2473 B.C., *i.e.,* the date of the Great Deluge. Geological evidence of this great catastrophe can still be found throughout the world. It profoundly changed the face of the earth and the life of man.

Some have also reasoned that the flood catastrophe even changed the speed of earth's rotation as well as its axial tilt. And there is some evidence to support such theories. By computing the time period mentioned in Genesis 8:3 & 4 it seems evident that the earth was on a 360-day solar cycle, instead of the 365.242 cycle which exists today. The law of kinetic energy ($\frac{1}{2}mv^2$) says that the rotation of a body increases as its mass decreases. With the vapor canopy surrounding the earth the rotation would be slower than after the water fell, because the transferring of the water to the surface of the earth would decrease the radial distance of the mass. It is probable that after the Deluge the length of the day would have decreased by twenty-one minutes, making five and one-quarter days more per orbit.

Whatever the fact or fancy, it is evident that the great flood catastrophe radically changed life here on this earth and shortened the life expectancy of man by half. This cataclysmic event was forever recorded in time by the alignment of stone 62 of the Bluestone Horseshoe.

To the right of stone 62 stands 63 in its original position. The alignment of this stone from the center intersects the Aubrey Circle at about the date-point 2202 ± B.C. According to some, this is said to be the approximate time of the patriarch Job, but we have no accurate chronological data concerning his year of birth or death. The significance of stone 63, therefore, must be left unsatisfied for the present.

Next in order is stone 34 of the Bluestone Circle, which still stands in its original position. A line drawn from the center across this stone intersects the Aubrey Circle at the important date-point of 2140 B.C. As discussed in Chapter 3, this was the date of the completion of the Great Pyramid.

Our attention is again drawn back to the Pyramid. The architect of Stonehenge seems to have been impressing upon our awareness the corresponding relationship of these two great monuments.

Stone 35 has been broken. A portion still stands in its original position, while a fragment of it lies between 9-10 of the Sarsen Circle. Since 34 pointed to the date of the erection of the Pyramid, perhaps 35 points to the date of the erection of Stonehenge. The alignment from center intersects the Aubrey Circle at the date-point 1973 B.C. This falls well within the time frame for the origin of Stonehenge. We offer this merely as conjecture here, but will discuss it in depth in Chapter 10.

The next stone to be considered is missing. The ground plans show it as having stood equidistant between 63 and 64 of the Bluestone Horseshoe. The alignment of this stone from the center gives a very important date in the history of man—especially in the history of the nation of Israel. The alignment intersects the Aubrey Circle at the date-point of 1814 B.C. The death of the patriarch Jacob occurred in the autumn of 1814 B.C. (Some chronologers suggest the spring of 1813 B.C.) Jacob died at the age of 147 years. Israel, as a nation, began at that time. It might be said that in autumn 1814 B.C. Jacob died and the nation of Israel was born.

According to Genesis 32:28 Jacob's name was changed to Israel: *"thy name shall be called no more Jacob, but Israel; for as a prince hast thou power with God and with men . . ."* Shortly before his death he pronounced a blessing upon each of his twelve sons. These twelve became the fathers of the twelve tribes of Israel. The year 1814 B.C. has gone down in the annals of mankind as the birth date of the nation of Israel.

Moving to the next stone of the horseshoe, 64, we find it to be merely a broken stub, barely visible above ground. It, too, marks a valuable link in the history of man—particularly the history of the nation of Israel. The alignment of Stone 64 from center intersects the Aubrey Circle at the date-point of 1569 B.C.

The people of Israel had been in bondage to the Pharoah of Egypt, but under the leadership of Moses they fled from Egypt and began their long journey to Canaan, which is now the land of Israel. Moses died before entering the land, and his successor as Israel's leader, Joshua, led the people across the Jordan river and into Canaan. Their God had promised this land to them, but first they had to conquer it and take it from the people who already inhabited it. The acquisition of the land took six years. Finally, by the spring of 1569 B.C. the land had been conquered and was apportioned to the twelve tribes of Israel, under the direction of Joshua. The Hebrew Scriptures give an account of this dividing of the land of Canaan in the book of Joshua, chapters 13 through 19. The twelve tribes of Israel now had a national home. The year was 1569 B.C.

The next stone to be considered is 36 of the Bluestone Circle. This stone has fallen to the ground. A line from the Sarsen Center across this stone intersects the Aubrey Circle at the date-point of 1462 B.C. A very interesting event in Jewish history occurred in that year. The nation of Israel had been conquered and placed under servitude to the king of Moab, whose name was Eglon, eighteen years prior to this, in 1480 B.C.* For eighteen years they had unwillingly served Eglon. (Judges 3:14)

A left-handed man of the tribe of Benjamin, named Ehud, delivered Israel from their bondage to Eglon. The story, as related in the book of Judges, is most interesting. Ehud went before the king with a present. But hidden under his clothes he carried a two-edged dagger. He placed the dagger on his right side. After presenting the gift to the king, he professed to have a secret message that only Eglon could hear. The people who had carried the present were sent away and Ehud and Eglon were left alone. Ehud reached with his left hand and drew the dagger from his right side and thrust it through the king. He locked the doors as he left the king's chamber and escaped back to his people. When the king's servants came and saw the closed door, they supposed he was relieving himself, so they

---

*The dates herein shown for the Judges of Israel are not always in agreement with other chronologers. This fact must exist because few chronologers are in agreement with each other in this era. Those who have graciously helped with the copy-reading and editing of this book do not agree with some of the dates shown here for the Judges. I must, however, present them according to my convictions.

waited politely outside the door, expecting that the king would open it when he had finished his private necessities. They waited and waited, until they were ashamed. Finally, they obtained a key and opened the door. Eglon was dead!

So Moab was subdued that day under the hand of Israel, and the land had rest four-score years. (Judges 3:30)

The year was 1462 B.C.

The next stone to the right, number 37, is leaning heavily, but has not fallen to the ground. A line from the center across this stone intersects the Aubrey Circle at the date-point 1315 B.C.—an interesting date indeed! The events which transpired that year had a profound effect upon the nation of Israel, and eventually, by implication, upon the whole world.

The nation of Israel had suffered in bondage and servitude to Midian for seven years. Finally the Midianites came up against Israel to destroy completely the land and the people. A man named Gideon, an Israelite of the tribe of Manasseh, was visited by an angel who instructed him to muster an army and make an attack upon Midian. Thirty-two thousand men of Israel responded to the call. But the angel told Gideon that this was too many; therefore all who were afraid to go to battle against the Midianites were instructed to return home. Twenty-two thousand returned, leaving a very small army of ten thousand. The angel said there were still too many, and instructed Gideon to bring them to a place of water and let them drink. Those who stooped down upon their knees to drink were also sent home, leaving a small band of three hundred men to go to battle against the innumerable host of Midianites. But the angel had a plan! Instead of weapons, each man was given a trumpet and an empty earthen pitcher in which a lamp was hidden. Silently, in the dark of night, they spread out over the hillsides which surrounded the valley where the Midianites were encamped, each man with his lamp burning but hidden, within the pitcher. When all were strategically positioned on the hillsides, Gideon gave a blast on his trumpet—a signal to his three hundred men. Then all blew on their trumpets and broke the earthen pitchers, letting the lamplight free. As they blew on the trumpets in their right hands and held the lamps high with their left hands, the sight and sound instilled terror in the camp of Midian. In the confusion they began killing each other, and attempted to flee for their life. Then Israelites from the tribes of Naphtali, Asher and Manasseh joined the three hundred and pursued after the fleeing host of Midian. Thus Israel was delivered from oppression, and had peace from their enemies for forty years.

This most remarkable battle was fought in the year 1315 B.C., but it has tremendous significance for all the world. This conflict is used in the Bible to illustrate an even greater, yet similar holocaust—the battle of Armageddon.

The next stone to be considered in order of its chronologic significance is number 65 of the Bluestone Horseshoe. Today it can be seen as merely a broken stub, barely rising above the ground level. Nevertheless it stands in its original position. The alignment of this stone from center intersects the Aubrey Circle at 1249 ± B.C. Very little is known regarding this date.

Moving to the next stone in chronological order, we come to stone 38 of the Bluestone Circle. This is one of the four stones of the circle composed of rhyolite. It still stands but leans heavily. A line drawn from the Sarsen Center across this stone will intersect the Aubrey Circle at the date-point of 1119 B.C. In June of 1119 B.C. the nation of Israel anointed their first king. Prior to this they had been ruled by judges. But desiring to be like other nations, they asked for a king. Samuel, their last judge, anointed Saul, a young handsome man of the tribe of Benjamin, to the position.

And Samuel said to all the people, see ye him whom the Lord hath chosen, that there is none like him among all the people? And all the people shouted, and said, God save the king. (1 Samuel 10:24)

This was the beginning of the Israelite monarchy which would continue for about 500 years.

Next in order is stone 66 of the Bluestone Horseshoe. Today it is merely a broken stub. It has been observed that this stone has a longitudinal protuberance with the same dimensions as

73

a groove that extends the full length of stone 68, its counterpart equidistant from the axis. Some British authors think that these two stones were once connected, but their is wide disagreement as to the reasonableness of such a theory. Some have suggested that they never were actually joined, but were tooled in this way to represent a symbolic joining.* Only conjecture is possible. Facts are not known. We will leave such conjecture to the archaeologists.

The alignment of stone 66 from the center intersects the Aubrey Circle at the date-point of 999 B.C., a tragic date in the history of the Israelite monarchy. It meant the dividing of the nation into the two-tribe kingdom and the ten-tribe kingdom.

Saul had not established a dynasty. Upon his death David, of the tribe of Judah, became king. David reigned in Israel forty years, and upon his death, his son Solomon was established upon the throne. Solomon's reign had been a prosperous one, and during his forty years on the throne of Israel the nation gained considerable fame. Following his death, his son Rehoboam became king. The year was 999 B.C.

Rehoboam, apparently somewhat arrogant and infused with a sense of his own power, made a proclamation that he would increase the burdens of the people. Because of his refusal to listen to his wise counsellors, the people rebelled against him and would no longer recognize him as their king. Only the tribes of Judah and Benjamin remained loyal. The other ten tribes established a rival monarchy and placed Jeroboam upon the throne. The schism was never to heal. Israel remained a divided nation until the ten-tribe kingdom was overthrown by Assyria in 722 B.C. and the two-tribe kingdom became a vassal to Babylon in 607 B.C.

Stone 39 of the Bluestone Circle is also leaning. A line drawn from the center across this stone will intersect the Aubrey Circle at about 938 ± B.C. Since chronology of this era is not clear, no attempt at interpretation will be given to this alignment.

---

*It has been suggested that stone 66 reveals it was once joined but eventually became separated, just as the Israelite monarchy under Saul, David and Solomon became a divided monarchy after the death of Solomon, never to be joined again.

Stone 40 of the Bluestone Circle is lying on the ground. It is of rhyolite. Using the ground plans which show its original position, a line drawn from the center across this stone would intersect the Aubrey Circle at about 847 ± B.C. Again, no attempt will be made to find the significance of this alignment.

Stone 67 of the Bluestone Horseshoe is next in chronologic order. It originally stood near the axis of symmetry, but now lies on the ground, probably knocked over by the fall of upright 55 and the lintel of the Great Trilithon. Its alignment from center intersects the Aubrey Circle at the date-point of 627 B.C. This is also the azimuth of winter solstice sunset, as viewed from the center through the Great Trilithon. As discussed in Chapter 2, 627 B.C. was a date with great significance, for it was not only the year of Israel's last possible Jubilee, but it also marked the mid-point in the 7,000-year cycle.

Stone 68 of the horseshoe is still intact, upright, and in its original position. A line drawn from the Sarsen Center across 68 will intersect the Aubrey Circle at the date-point of 264 B.C. This was the year of the First Punic War, *i.e.*, the war between Rome and Carthage. It marked the beginning of Roman expansion which eventually covered all of western Europe. By 148 B.C. Roman expansion had also included Macedonia and the east. The Greek empire became subservient to Rome. In the course of little more than a century Rome had become the supreme power of the civilized world. It was Rome who not only held the seat of civil power, but eventually would also hold the seat of ecclesiastical power under the authority of the papacy.

That this date, 264 B.C., should be marked by a bluestone alignment is significant, for it was the beginning of events which would dominate the whole of the civilized world for over two thousand years.

Ground plans show that a stone once stood between 68 and 69. No stone is there today. We will designate this missing stone by the number 68A. A line drawn from the center of the Sarsen Circle across the mid-point of the spot where this stone once stood will intersect the Aubrey Circle at the date-point of 2 B.C., the date of the birth of Jesus. It is not surprising that such an event which changed the course of history would be marked by a bluestone alignment. There has been controversy among historians regarding the actual date of Jesus' birth. An in-depth discussion of this subject will be found in Appendix V. For purposes of brevity here, we will only state the conviction that his date of birth was September 29, 2 B.C., which, according to Jewish reckoning, was the first day of their month Tishri—their New Year Day, Rosh Hashanah, the day of the Feast of Trumpets.

The stone next to be considered stands all alone in the Bluestone Circle. In fact, it does not even stand. Today it lies prone. It is number 41. A line drawn from the Sarsen Center across this stone intersects the Aubrey Circle at the date-point of 33 A.D., the date of the death of Jesus. As already mentioned, this is the azimuth of the Passover moonrise. It was not by coincidence that Jesus died on the afternoon of Passover; nor was it coincidence that the Passover moon eclipsed at the hour of his death (Greenwich Time). Just so, it was not by coincidence that the azimuth of Passover moonrise at Stonehenge should intersect the Aubrey Circle at the date-point of (spring) 33 A.D. Jesus died April 3, 33 A.D.

Stonehenge—that wonderful monument which stands as solitary in history as on the great plain—knows no place for coincidence!

Moving to the next stone of the horseshoe, we find 69 still standing in its original position. A line drawn from the center across this stone will intersect the Aubrey Circle at the date-point of 312 A.D. On October 28, 312 A.D., Constantine defeated Maxentius at the Milvain Bridge on the Tiber. He then entered Rome as the sole master of the western half of the empire. To commemorate his victory he erected the triumphal Arch of Constantine. In 313 he issued the famous Edict of Milan which gave Christians the right to practice their religion openly. Constantine was the first Christian emperor of Rome. By 323 he had brought the entire Roman world under his rule.

A controversy raged among Christians. Arius, of Alexandria, maintained that Christ was not the equal of the Father but was created by Him. Athanasius, leader of the bishops in the west, claimed that the Father and Son, though distinct, are equal, and of the same substance. To settle the matter, Constantine called together, in 325, a world-wide council of bishops at Nicaea. He himself presided over the assembly. An overwhelming majority condemned the Arian view as heresy. The Council drew up the Nicene Creed, which is still accepted in most Christian churches today.

Next to the right of 69 stands 70, in its original position. A line from the Sarsen Center across this stone will intersect the Aubrey Circle at the date-point of 555 A.D. It was in 555 A.D. that the Gothic nation was finally and completely subdued and brought under subjection to Justinian I.* As mentioned in Chapter 4, the azimuth of winter moonset low as viewed through the Moonset Trilithon gave the date 539 which saw the beginning of papal power in Rome. This came about by the overthrow of the Ostrogothic kingdom in Italy. However, the kernel of that nation was not at that time brought into subjection. In 552 re-conquest was attempted. By 555 the Goths were completely defeated and Italy was annexed. The people were now brought under papal authority.

The next stone to be considered is 42 of the Bluestone Circle. Today it lies prone. Considering its original position, a line drawn from the Sarsen Center across this stone will intersect the Aubrey Circle at the date-point of 800 A.D. It was on Christmas day 800 A.D. that Pope Leo III took a golden crown from off the altar and placed it on the head of Charlemagne. The people in the church shouted, "To Charles the August, crowned by God, great and pacific emperor, long life and victory." The coronation of Charlemagne was the foundation of the Holy Roman Empire. Though Charlemagne did not use the title, he is considered the first Holy Roman emperor. Thus the year 800 marks the beginning of the Holy Roman Empire which was to continue until its final abolition in 1806. Upon Charlemagne's death the breakup of the Frankish kingdom was nearly a death blow to the empire, which disappeared for

---

*Some historians give 554 for this event. The bluestone alignments allow a one or two year variance, for it is not always possible to determine accurately the precise center point of the stone in its original position.

a time, but was revived and given new strength and power by Otto the Great in 962. As mentioned in Chapter 4, the azimuth of summer solstice sunset as viewed through the Sunset Trilithon clearly marks the date of 962. It meant the survival of the empire.

Next to be considered is a missing stone of the horseshoe. We will designate it 71A. A line from the Sarsen Center across the spot where it once stood will intersect the Aubrey Circle at the date-point of 918 A.D. As discussed in Chapter 4, in August of 918 Conrad I of Germany, upon his death bed, named Henry I (Henry the Fowler) to be his successor to the crown. This bluestone alignment intersects the Aubrey Circle at the same date-point as the azimuth of winter moonset high as viewed through the Moonset Trilithon. The rule of Henry I was the beginning of the Saxon dynasty in Germany, and the beginning of an official church-state system which was to rule Germany for many centuries. It was the Saxon dynasty which saved the papacy from disaster. Henry's son, Otto the Great, became emperor of the Holy Roman Empire in 962, reviving the empire from near extinction.

We move now to stone 43 of the Bluestone Circle. It is lying on the ground. A line drawn from the Sarsen Center across the spot where this stone once stood upright will intersect the Aubrey Circle at the date-point of 1184 A.D. The Council of Verona in 1184 saw the institution of the inquisition against heretics. It was there that Pope Lucius III and the emperor Frederick I agreed upon the penalties for heresy, *i.e.,* exile, confiscation, demolition of houses, and loss of civil rights. This paved the way for the infliction of the death penalty in 1197. It was during this period that the pope's function of "vicar of St. Peter" gradually came to be changed to "vicar of Christ." the claim was of immeasurable value, for it greatly increased the papal authority. Recalcitrant bishops who might maintain that they were the equals of the pope and that he therefore could not give them orders were thus reduced to silence. Since Christ was held to have been both King and Priest from whom all power stemmed (an axiom to which everyone adhered), his vicar too asserted the same combination of offices in his person, with the consequences that he, like Christ, claimed all power.

The next stone of the Bluestone Horseshoe is missing. We will designate it 71B. A line drawn from the Sarsen Center across the spot where this stone once stood will intersect the Aubrey Circle at the date-point of 1309 A.D. This year marked the beginning of the decline of the Holy Roman Empire and of the papacy. It was in 1309 that pope Clement V, under pressure from Philip IV, of France, moved his residence from Rome to Avignon. This later became known as the "Babylonian Captivity" of the papacy, for it lasted about 70 years. It has also been called the "dawn of the Reformation," for it was out of the decline of the empire that the roots of reformation began to take life. At Munich a new wave of antipapal argument and propaganda came into being, encouraged by the revolutionary thinking of Marsilius (Marsiglio) of Padua. An intellectual attack upon the pope was pressed by Occam, whose polemical works taught that the papacy under John XXII did not possess Christian teaching, but was, in fact, heretical.

The internal decay of the papacy resulted, in 1378, in the Great Schism. The division led to the election of two rival popes. In 1409 an attempt was made to heal the schism by electing a new pope. The result was merely that now, instead of two, they had three. The Great Schism caused Wycliffe to come out as a reformer. Clearly the decline of papal power was never to heal.

The next stone to be considered is number 44 of the Bluestone Circle. Today it lies prone. A line drawn from the Sarsen Center across the spot where this stone once stood upright will intersect the Aubrey Circle at the date-point of 1356 A.D. In the year 1356, Charles IV, of Germany, issued the Golden Bull. It made the empire, in theory, elective, creating an Electoral College. The result was simply that the election of a king became the responsibility of the state, and removed any authority of appointment or confirmation from the pope. This was a serious blow to the power of the papacy, which was already in the throes of decadence.

79

The next stone to be considered is number 45 of the Blue-stone Circle. It, too, lies on the ground. A line drawn from the Sarsen Center across the spot where this stone originally stood will intersect the Aubrey Circle at the date-point of 1517 A.D. It was the memorable year of 1517 when Martin Luther nailed his 95 theses to the door of the Wittenberg church. It created no small stir! In 1520 the pope issued a bull, or proclamation, condemning the "hersey" of Luther's teachings. Luther publicly burned the bull in Wittenberg and continued teaching and writing. It was the beginning of a mortal wound to the power of the papacy in Germany and throughout most of Europe.

That the year 1517 should be marked by a bluestone alignment at Stonehenge is not surprising, for it began the Great Reformation which divided the Christian world into two major camps, *i.e.,* Catholic and Protestant.

The stone next to be considered is number 71 of the Blue-stone Horseshoe. Today it lies on the ground. A line from the center across the spot where this stone once stood upright will intersect the Aubrey Circle at the date-point of 1545 A.D. This marked the year of the attempt at Counter-Reformation by the papacy. The Council of Trent convened in 1545. Its purpose was to quell the tide of the Protestant Reformation and to re-establish the supremacy of the pope. It enjoyed a measure of success; however the inroads of Protestantism had been firmly established and could not be stopped. By the end of the 16th century the effect of the Counter-Reformation could be seen. The church had regained the faith of the people in half the lands it had lost to Protestantism. Europe was then divided between these two forms of Christianity by almost the same lines that exist today.

The next stone of the horseshoe, number 72, is also lying on the ground. A line drawn from the center across the spot where it once stood will intersect the Aubrey Circle at the date-point of 1799 A.D. That year saw the destruction of the temporal authority of the papacy. The French Revolution, which had begun in 1789, was bringing great changes to France. In 1799 pope Pius VI was taken prisoner by Napoleon, and there he died. The papacy had also suffered a fatal wound. In 1804 when Napoleon was crowned emperor of France, he took the crown from the hands of pope Pius VII and placed it on his own head. He boldly ignored both the blessings and curses of the papacy. His phenomenal success completely weakened the papal influence over civil governments. In 1806 the Holy Roman Empire came to an end.

There remains one more bluestone of the horseshoe and four more of the circle. The dates to which these point are all future from the time of this writing. The alignments of these stones will be discussed in Chapter 11, Prophecy.

The bluestones have given us a record of the history of man. But more particularly they have given us a record of man's relationship with his Creator. The bluestones, like a giant clock, have recorded the time. They have recorded it accurately. How did the builder of Stonehenge know the important events of history before those events ever came into being? Or did he? Why were those bluestones placed so carefully and so accurately as to tell the time for thousands of years in advance?

Surely time is powerless against truth. Though all else may suffer the inevitable results of entropy and decay, yet truth remains. Euripides was right. "Time will discover everything to posterity."

STONEHENGE...A CLOSER LOOK

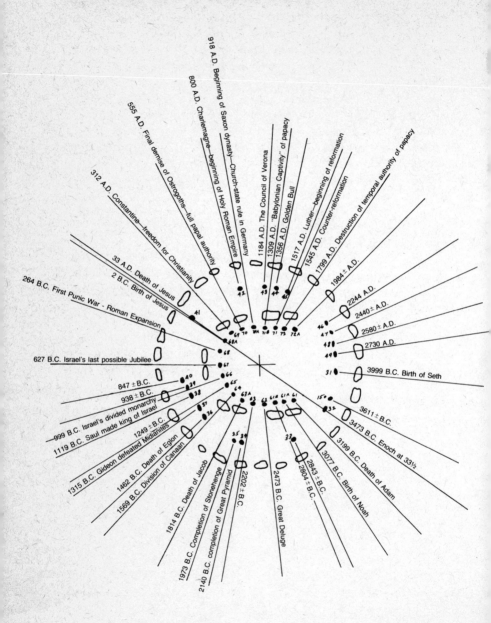

918 A.D. Beginning of Saxon dynasty—Church-state rule in Germany

800 A.D. Charlemagne—beginning of Holy Roman Empire

555 A.D. Final demise of Ostrogoths—full papal authority

312 A.D. Constantine—freedom for Christianity

33 A.D. Death of Jesus

2 B.C. Birth of Jesus

264 B.C. First Punic War - Roman Expansion

627 B.C. Israel's last possible Jubilee

847 ± B.C.

938 ± B.C.

999 B.C. Israel's divided monarchy

1119 B.C. Saul made king of Israel

1249 ± B.C.

1315 B.C. Gideon defeated Midianites

1462 B.C. Death of Eglon

1569 B.C. Division of Canaan

1814 B.C. Death of Jacob

1973 B.C. Completion of Stonehenge

2140 B.C. completion of Great Pyramid

2202 ± B.C.

2473 B.C. Great Deluge

2804 ± B.C.

2843 ± B.C.

3077 B.C. Birth of Noah

3199 B.C. Death of Adam

3473 B.C. Enoch at 33½

3611 ± B.C.

3999 B.C. Birth of Seth

2730 A.D.

2580 ± A.D.

2440 ± A.D.

2244 A.D.

1984 ± A.D.

1799 A.D. Destruction of temporal authority of papacy

1545 A.D. Counter-reformation

1517 A.D. Luther—beginning of reformation

1356 A.D. Golden Bull

1309 A.D. "Babylonian Captivity" of papacy

1184 A.D. The Council of Verona

82

6

The Meridian

"I am as constant as the Northern star, of whose true-fixed and resting quality there is no fellow in the firmament."
—Shakespeare

Perhaps the northern star appeared to be a constant to Shakespeare, but in fact, it is not. The star to which he referred was probably Polaris. Since it is the nearest star to the celestial pole today, we think of it as stationary. The true celestial pole is indeed a constant, however. The celestial meridian is the great circle of the celestial sphere which passes through its poles and the observer's zenith. The terrestrial meridian is the great circle of the earth which passes through the poles and any given point on the earth's surface.

Come with me to Stonehenge on the day of summer solstice. The sun is bright and not veiled by clouds. As we walk through those towering monoliths we observe an interesting shadow pattern. The huge stones of the Moonrise Trilithon (53-54) are so positioned as to cause the sun to cast a streak of light on the ground which passes through the slot. It is a very thin streak of light, and as the sun continues to climb to the zenith, the streak dwindles to a fine line and finally disappears. At that moment the sun is over the meridian of Stonehenge. It is apparent noon, and the fine line has precisely marked the north-south direction. This meridian does not, however, pass through the Sarsen Center nor the Aubrey Center, though it is close to both.*

The points at which this meridian intersect the Aubrey Circle are startling! Pointing directly south the point of inter-

---

*Fernand Niel, *The Mysteries of Stonehenge*, Avon Books, New York, 1974, p. 194.

section is 129.16° from summer solstice sunrise, and pointing north it intersects the circle at 308.78°. By the formula explained in Chapter 2, these can be translated into two very interesting dates. The south point of intersection becomes the year (spring) 1615 B.C. while the north point of intersection is 1878 A.D. But why these two dates?

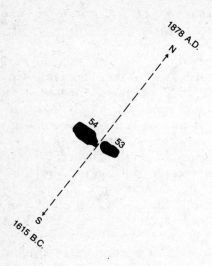

Figure 25

After the Israelites fled from the slavery and oppression in Egypt, under the leadership of Moses they experienced a miraculous deliverance through the Red Sea. Soon after their safe arrival on the other side, Moses was called up into Mount Sinai and there he received the Ten Commandments. It was the spring of 1615 B.C. This fine line of sunlight that proceeds from the slot of the Moonrise Trilithon is pointing directly to the date of the Mosaic Law.

The fact that the Moonrise Trilithon is used for this purpose is also significant, for throughout the Bible the moon is symbolic of the Mosaic Law. It is not surprising to find at Stonehenge, the use of this symbol also.

The northerly direction of this meridian intersects the Aubrey Circle at the date-point of 1878 A.D.—a most significant date in the history of the people of Israel.

Anti-Semitism had been rampant throughout most of Europe and the Near East. However, a Jew had risen to the position of Prime Minister in England. His name was Benjamin Disraeli—better known to the world as Lord Beaconsfield. He represented England at the Berlin Congress of Nations of 1878. Disraeli had a plan whereby the Jews could have access to their ancient homeland, which had become known as the land of Palestine. A memorandum which he had prepared to present to the Congress was printed in the Vienna press under the title *"Die Jüdische Frage in der Orientalischen Frage"* (The Jewish Question in the Oriental Question). Anticipating the sure collapse of the Ottoman Empire which ruled the land, Disraeli suggested to the Congress that the Jews should obtain Palestine and establish there a state of their own under the protectorate of Great Britain. Disraeli was a far-sighted man for he asked, "Is it not probable that within, say, half a century, there would be developed in that land a compact Jewish people, one million strong, speaking one language, and animated by one spirit—the desire to achieve autonomy and independence?"

In 1878 the first Jewish settlers in Palestine began arriving from Russia. By 1882 the first colony had been established. They named it *Petach Tikva* (Door of Hope) in fulfillment of the ancient promise: *"I will give her her vineyards from thence, and the valley of Achor for a door of hope; and she shall sing there, as in the days of her youth, and as in the day when she came up out of the land of Egypt."* (Hosea 2:15)

Disraeli's dream of Jewish autonomy within half a century was not quite realized. Seventy years after 1878, on May 14, 1948, the modern state of Israel was born.

This unusual view of Stonehenge is taken along the line of its central axis. The Heel Stone can be seen in the distance (center). Note the enormous stone of the Great Central Trilithon with its tenon "knob" protruding from the top. This tenon once fit securely into a corresponding groove in the lintel which rested upon it.

7

The Amazing Sarsen Circle

Stonehenge, in Wiltshire in the south of England, is in many respects an engineering and mathematical marvel. It is not situated on a hilltop nor in a valley but on a broad plain which slopes gently toward the northeast and the Avon. Nevertheless, the top surface of the ring of lintels which forms the crown of the Sarsen Circle is level. It has been suggested by some authors that this crown of lintels came the closest to perfection of any other feature of the monument. Fernand Niel suggested that perhaps the sun god, when looking down, would be able to behold this flawless circle which represented him. Call him a sun god if you will, but the Creator of the universe is, in fact, represented by the perfect geometric figure—a circle.

This perfection of the upper surface of the lintels cannot be appreciated by one standing on the ground. The terrestrial viewer gets the impression that the circle is uneven. This is due to the natural unevenness of the ground. The heights of the stones were planned to compensate for this.

The Sarsen Circle was originally composed of thirty upright stones, joined at their tops by thirty lintels. Petrie took measurements of the uprights that were still in place, and found that the heights varied from 12 feet 8 inches to 14 feet 6 inches; a difference of 1 foot 10 inches. Therefore Petrie suggested the average height for the uprights to be 13 feet 6 inches, even though only one upright, number 7, actually has that height.

Even the suggestion of an average height detracts from the beautiful fact of their evenness at the top and their unevenness at the bottom.

Dimensions given for the uprights by various authors are all approximate, with a great margin of error because the stones are not sharp and regular enough to permit precision. The lintels of the Sarsen Circle, however, were the most regularly shaped of all the stones in the monument. They were carefully tooled to form a gentle curve. The precision with which they were curved is an engineering marvel for, when joined, they formed a perfect circle. Any unevenness in the tops of the uprights was offset by the thickness of the lintels, making their upper surface level.

Lest we tend to overlook the marvelous engineering ability of the builder, let us remember that those perfectly shaped lintels were tooled before being lifted into place; that they were not only curved to form a perfect circle, but were also given mortise holes on their under sides to fit over corresponding tenons atop each upright, and were given tongue-and-groove fittings at each end. Those 7 ton boulders were tooled and shaped at the quarry, some 20 miles away; cut-and-fit methods were not used. The stones had to be shaped accurately before the laborious task of lifting them into place could be started. The precision with which the level, perfect circle was accomplished, by men working without modern technology or sophisticated tools, is staggering to our powers of comprehension.

Before constructing the circle its circumference or diameter must be known. Which of these was decided beforehand? Which was the most important to the bulder? To the modern mind it may seem perhaps a foolish question, for we deal with circles in terms of radius or diameter. But remember that the one who designed that circle also had the task of dividing it into 30 equal parts, without precision instruments or trigonometric tables. It might be supposed that a method of successive approximations was used until reasonable accuracy was achieved, but the precision with which the lintels were shaped rules out any such trial-and-error approximations. Since all

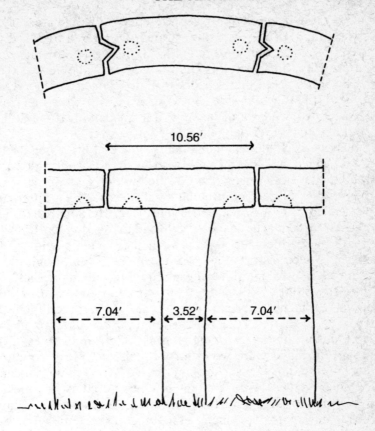

Figure 26

shaping and tooling had to be done before they were lifted into place, their length and curvature had to be known accurately in advance. The builder had to know the function of π and had to know that 12° divisions of the circle would give 30 equal parts. The precision with which the lintels were placed, and the accuracy of the division of the circle into 30 equal parts is awesome when we consider the time and circumstances under which that marvelous old monument was built.

STONEHENGE...A CLOSER LOOK

The ratio between the circumference and diameter of a circle, called π (pi) was demonstrated by the building of the Great Pyramid, which preceded the building of Stonehenge, therefore it is clear that this knowledge was available.

The inner faces of the stones of the Sarsen Circle were shown by Petrie to be tangent to a circle with a diameter of 97.3 feet. Allowing for the average thickness of the stones, this would give an outer diameter of about 105.6 feet.

In 1924 E. H. Stone, an engineer, looked at those beautiful lintels which had been made with such precision and was awed by the engineering savvy of the builder. He approached the problem of determining the circumference by a different method from that which Petrie had used. He noted that the lintels were so placed that each one had three equal portions—one third spanned the gap between the uprights, while the other two sections extended to the centers of the uprights on either side. Thus one-third of each lintel rested on one-half of an upright; one-third spanned the gap; and one-third rested on half of the next upright. The average gap between the pillars is 3.52 feet. Thus the average length of the lintels is 10.56 feet. This is not, however, the length of their inner faces, it is the mean. Since there were thirty lintels, the mean circumference would have been 10.56 x 30 = 316.8 feet, giving a mean diameter of 100.84 feet. That the builder should use the mean is thrilling, for the figure 316.8 is loaded with meaning. Using the mean was also a geometrical method of shortening the circumference of the circle in order that it would be three times the diameter. It is evident that the builder used the mean by the geometry and gematria which its numbers provide.

Measures

Before experiencing the world of geometry and gematria displayed by the Sarsen Circle, it is first necessary to ask, what was the unit of measure used by the builder? At the Great Pyramid it has been observed that a unit known as the Pyramid Inch was used, as well as other well known units. At Stonehenge it appears that several units of measure can be used, and probably were used by the builder, for they are all in harmony with its geometry. Most of them are probably familiar to the reader. A. Thom, in his studies of Stonehenge, suggested yet another, *i.e.*, the megalithic yard (MY = 2.72 feet). The megalithic yard, as Thom found to be used at Stonehenge, is also an essential component of Egyptian measures.

The best known of Egyptian measures is the royal cubit of 1.72 feet and the remen of 1.2165 feet. These two are related in that a square with sides of one remen has a diagonal of one royal cubit. Two other linear units are the Palestinian cubit of 2.107 feet and the Roman pace of 2.433 feet. All of these are related to one another.

1.2165 feet = 1 remen
1.72 feet = 1 royal cubit
2.107 feet = 1 Palestinian cubit
2.4333 feet = 1 Roman pace
2.72 feet = 1 megalithic yard (MY)
660 feet = 1 furlong
5,280 feet = 1 mile
14,400 feet (2.727272 miles) = 1 megalithic mile (MMi)

1 remen x $\sqrt{2}$ = 1 royal cubit
1 remen x $\sqrt{3}$ = 1 Palestinian cubit
1 remen x $\sqrt{4}$ = 1 Roman pace
1 remen x $\sqrt{5}$ = 1 megalithic yard (MY)
1 remen x $\sqrt{6}$ = 1 yard (approx.)

1 square remen   = .74 x 2 (square feet)
1 square royal cubit   = .74 x 4 (square feet)
1 square Palestinian cubit = .74 x 6 (square feet)
1 square Roman pace   = .74 x 8 (square feet)
1 square megalithic yard   = .74 x 10 (square feet)
1 square yard   = .74 x 12 (square feet)

The numerical equivalent of the Greek spelling of Creation, κτιοις, or Circle, κυκλος, is 740. Thus these measures which are used to define the circles of Stonehenge are part of the units of creation.

The megalithic mile was observed by John Michell* to be identical to an ancient unit which is still in use in the far East, called the *pu*. It is called the megalithic mile because its ratio to the English mile is virtually the same as the megalithic yard to the English foot. The cosmological relationship between the megalithic mile and the English mile is remarkable.

Diameter of the earth	=	7,920 English miles
Diameter of the moon	=	792 megalithic miles
Perimeter of a square containing the circle of the earth	=	31,680 English miles
Perimeter of a square containing the circle of the moon	=	3,168 megalithic miles
Diameter of the sun	=	316,800 megalithic miles
(Mean circumference of the Sarsen Circle	=	316.8 feet)

From time immemorial the circumference of the earth (and circles) has been divided into 360 degrees or 21,600 minutes, and time is similarly measured. The diameter of the moon is 2,160 miles. Each of the 360 degrees around the earth's circumference measures 365,242 feet,† which is the number of days in a thousand years.

The prophetic *"time"* of the Hebrew Scriptures is 360 days = 1 year; or, 1 *"time"* = 360 years. 6 x 360 = 2160, or the diameter of the moon. The radius of the moon is therefore 1080 miles. In metrology 1080 feet = 888 remens, and 888 is the gematria for the name of Jesus, 'Ιησους. Also, 1080 square megalithic yards is equal to 888 square yards. The area of the Sarsen Circle is 1080 square megalithic yards or 888 square yards. Thus it becomes apparent that the ancient units of linear measure, and time, are all related to one another and

---

*John Michell, *City of Revelation*, Ballantine Books, New York, p. 119

†The round figure of 7920 miles is generally used for the mean diameter of the earth. However, the mathematically accurate figure is 7926.8, giving a mean circumference of 24,902.8. Thus 24,092.8 x 5280 ÷ 360 = 365,242

are, in addition, related to the Bible, Stonehenge and the universe.

The modern metric system, on the other hand, is related to none of these. It was contrived by man to represent one ten-millionth part of the length of a quadrant of the meridian through Paris, but it is not, in fact, commensurate with the universe and therefore is totally unsuitable for archaeological work and the measuring of antiquities.

Geometry and Gematria

Gematria is the cryptographic significance of words, revealing their hidden meaning. It was employed by the Greeks and the Hebrews. The system is quite simple. The characters of both the Greek and Hebrew alphabets were given numerical equivalents; thus, any word, name or phrase had a corresponding number. The geometry of Stonehenge and the gematria of the Bible have a remarkable relationship. It is a relationship which expands to include the geometry of the universe and the chronology of the ages.

The beautiful ring of lintels which topped the Sarsen Circle staggers the imagination. They were tooled and dressed with precision and placed into position with an expertise far beyond our comprehension. The mean circumference of these lintels is 316.8 feet—the number which identifies the Lord Jesus Christ, Κυριος Ιησους Χριστος. When the circumference is measured in megalithic yards it becomes 116.4 MY. The gematria for Son of God, υιος θεον, is 1164. The interval between the uprights is 3.52 feet. Jesus said *"I am the Way."* The numerical equivalent for *"the Way,"* η οδος, is 352. The perimeter of a square drawn on the extreme circumference of the Sarsen Circle is 140.8 yards. The gematria for Savior, σωτηρ, is 1408. The Sarsen Circle is thus related to the Savior of the world.

This relationship is demonstrated in many ways. The fact that there were originally thirty uprights in the Sarsen Circle, as well as thirty lintels, also relates to Jesus. It was at thirty years of age that he presented himself to John to be baptized—

93

a symbol of the sacrifice of his humanity on behalf of all mankind. The number thirty represents perfection as well as completion.

The number thirty also plays an important role in the relationship of the Sarsen Circle to the Great Pyramid. Thirty times the height of the stones (from ground to upper surface of the lintels) is equal to the height of the Pyramid from its socket level base to the apex. To demonstrate that this relationship is no coincidence, it is worth noting also that ten times the inner circumference of the Sarsen Circle is equal to the perimeter of the Great Pyramid at its socket level.

That the Sarsen Circle is identified with Jesus is further shown by the gematria of his name, for Jesus, 'Ιησους, is 888. The mean area of the Sarsen Circle is 888 square yards. Three times this number (3 x 888) is 2664. The inner circumference of the Sarsen Circle has an area of .0002664 square miles. The area of a square drawn on the extreme circumference of the Sarsen Circle is .0256 square furlongs or .256 acres. The distance from the center of the Sarsen Circle to the base of the Heel Stone is 256 feet. Jesus said *"I am the Way, the Truth and the Life."* Truth, αληθης, is 256. The area of the Sarsen Circle on its mean circumference is 2699 royal cubits. The gematria for *"I am the Resurrection and the life,"* 'Εγω ειμι η αναστασις και η ζων, is 2698.*

Jesus was called by many titles and it is not surprising to find that their gematria corresponds to the numbers of the Sarsen Circle. To his disciples he was known as the Master, ο διδασκαλος, which is 586. The mean diameter of the Sarsen Circle is 58.6 royal cubits. To the common people he was known as the Rabbi, ο ραββι, 185. The mean radius of the Sarsen Circle is 18.5 MY while a square drawn on the inner face of the Sarsen Circle measures 185 Palestinian cubits.

When Jesus came to John at the river Jordan to be baptized, John said, *"Behold the Lamb of God."* Lamb, αρνιον, is 281. One side of a square whose perimeter equals the circumfer-

---

*In gematria one unit, known as colel, may be added to or subtracted from the value of any word without affecting its meaning.

ence of the inner face of the Sarsen Circle is 28.1 MY while the area of that square is .0000281 square MMi.

He was known to many as Jesus of Nazareth, Ἰησου Ναζωραιον, 1777. The circumference of the inner face of the Sarsen Circle is 177.7 royal cubits, while the distance from the Sarsen Center to the base of the Heel Stone is .01777 MMi. Or sometimes he was simply called the Nazarene, Ναζωραιος, 1239. The area of a square drawn on the outer face of the Sarsen Circle is 1239 square yards. Those who accepted him as the fulfillment of the prophetic Messiah called him Christ, Χριστος, which is the Greek spelling for Messiah. The gematria for Christ is 1480. There are 1480 square Roman paces in the area enclosed within the outer face of the Sarsen Circle. Those who were close to him called him Lord, Κυριος, 800, and there are .0800 furlongs in the radius of the outer face of the Sarsen Circle.

In John 10 is recorded a beautiful illustration of Jesus' care and compassion for his followers. He said, *"I am the Good Shepherd, and know my sheep, and am known of mine."* The Good Shepherd, ο καλος ποιμην, is 649, while the area of a square whose perimeter is the same as the circumference of the inner face of the Sarsen Circle is 649 square yards. If we remove the definite article, Good Shepherd, καλος ποιμην, becomes 579. The circumference of the inner face of the Sarsen Circle is .0579 miles.

The Apostle Paul, in I Timothy 2:5 said, *"There is one God, and one mediator between God and men, the man Christ Jesus."* Mediator, μεσιτης, is 763, and there are .076393 furlongs in the mean radius of the Sarsen Circle as well as .76393 miles in the perimeter of a square drawn on the mean Sarsen Circle. His work as Mediator will be when he becomes the Bridegroom of his faithful church. The Bridegroom, ο νυμφιον, is 1340. The area of a square whose perimeter is the same as the circumference of the inner face of the Sarsen Circle is .01340 square furlongs or .1340 acres.

One of the beautiful prophecies in the Hebrew Scriptures concerning the future work of Jesus in bringing life and peace to the perishing human race is found in Isaiah 9:6, 7.

"For unto us a child is born, unto us a son is given: and the government shall be upon his shoulder: and his name shall be called Wonderful Counsellor, the mighty God, The Everlasting Father, The Prince of Peace. Of the increase of his government and peace there shall be no end, upon the throne of David, and upon his kingdom, to order it, and to establish it with judgment and with justice from henceforth even for ever."

He is said to be the *"Everlasting Father"* of mankind because he will father them with everlasting life. This loving, intimate and compassionate title, Father, Ηατερα, is by gematria 487 and there are 48.7 feet in the radius of the inner face of the Sarsen Circle.

The prophet Jeremiah spoke of the time when Jesus would reign in a kingdom of peace, and he called him by the beautiful name, Jehovah Tsidkenu, which by interpretation is "the righteousness of Jehovah." The text reads:

"Behold, the days come, saith the Lord, that I will raise unto David a righteous Branch, and a King shall reign and prosper, and shall execute judgment and justice in the earth … and this is the name whereby he shall be called, Jehovah Tsidkenu." (Jeremiah 23:5, 6)

This name, which describes a righteousness like unto the Creator himself, Jehovah Tsidkenu, יהוה צדקנו , is 276. There are 27.6 yards in one side of a square whose perimeter equals the circumference of the outer face of the Sarsen Circle. And interesting to note is the fact that there are roughly 27,600,000 furlongs in the perimeter of a square drawn on the circumference of the sun.

In the face of such overwhelming evidence, can there be any doubt that those 30-ton boulders forming the beautiful Sarsen Circle are telling us about Jesus! By geometry and gematria they tell the story of his birth, his baptism, his ministry, and his great future work of bringing life to all mankind. *"Of the increase of his government and peace there shall be no end."*

3168 = Lord Jesus Christ, Κυριος Ιησους Χριστος
316.8 feet—mean circumference of Sarsen Circle

1164 = Son of God, υιος Θεου
116.4 MY—mean circumference of Sarsen Circle

352 = The Way, η οδος
3.52 feet—interval between Sarsen uprights
35.2 yards—diameter of outer face of Sarsen Circle
    352 yards—circumference of outer face of Inner Bank

1408 = Savior, σωτηρ
140.8 yards—perimeter of a square drawn on the outer face
  of Sarsen Circle

888 = Jesus, Ιησους
888 square yards—mean area of Sarsen Circle
    .00888 square furlongs—area of a square of same
      perimeter as Bluestone Circle
    .0888 acres—area of a square of same perimeter as
      Bluestone Circle

256 = Truth, αληθης
.0256 square furlongs—area of a square drawn on outer face
  of Sarsen Circle
.256 acres—area of a square drawn on outer face of Sarsen
  Circle
256 feet—distance from Sarsen Center to base of Heel Stone
    .0000256 square MMi—area of Bluestone Circle
    25.6 Roman paces—one side of a square of same
      perimeter as Bluestone Circle
    25.6 remens—one side of a square of same perimeter as
      Bluestone Horseshoe

STONEHENGE...A CLOSER LOOK

264 = The Truth, η αληθης
26.4 yards—one side of a square of same perimeter as mean
   Sarsen Circle
 264 square Roman paces—area of a square drawn on
  Bluestone Horseshoe
 264 feet—one side of a square of same perimeter as
  outer face of Inner Bank
 264 feet—long side of Station Stone rectangle
 26.4 yards—diameter of Bluestone Circle

586 = Master, ο διδασκαλος
58.6 royal cubits—mean diameter of Sarsen Circle

185 = Rabbi, ο ραββι
185 Palestinian cubits—perimeter of a square drawn on inner
   face of Sarsen Circle
18.5 MY—mean radius of Sarsen Circle
 185 royal cubits—diameter of crest of Inner Bank
 .00185 square miles—area of a square of same perimeter
  as Aubrey Circle

281 = Lamb, αρνιον
28.1 MY—one side of a square of same perimeter as inner
   face of Sarsen Circle
.0000281 square MMi—area of a square of same perimeter
   as inner face of Sarsen Circle

1777 = Jesus of Nazareth, 'Ιησου Ναζωραιον
177.7 royal cubits—circumference of inner face of Sarsen
   Circle
.01777 MMi—distance from Sarsen Center to base of
   Heel Stone

1239 = Nazarene (Nazarite), Ναζωραιος
1239 square yards—area of a square drawn on outer face of
   Sarsen Circle

1480 = Christ (Messiah), Χριστος
1480 square Roman paces—area of outer face of Sarsen
  Circle

800 = Lord, Κυριος
.0800 furlongs—radius of outer face of Sarsen Circle
     .0800 MMi—perimeter of a square drawn on Aubrey
        Circle

649 = The Good Shepherd, ο καλος ποιμην
649 square yards—area of a square of same perimeter as
  inner face of Sarsen Circle

579 = Good Shepherd, καλος ποιμην
.0579 miles—circumference of inner face of Sarsen Circle

763 = Mediator, μεσιτης
.076393 furlongs—radius of mean Sarsen Circle
.076393 miles—perimeter of a square drawn on mean
  Sarsen Circle
764 square yards—area of a square of same perimeter as
  outer face of Sarsen Circle
76.4 feet—one side of a square of same perimeter as inner
  face of Sarsen Circle
     76,380,089 royal cubits—circumference of earth

1340 = Bridegroom, ο νυμφιου
.01340 square furlongs—area of a square of same perimeter
  as inner face of Sarsen Circle
.1340 acres—area of a square of same perimeter as inner face
  of Sarsen Circle

487 = Father, Πατερα
48.7 feet—radius of inner face of Sarsen Circle
     .000487 square MMi—area of a square drawn on crest
        of Inner Bank

276 = Jehovah Tsidkenu, יהוה צדקנו
27.6 yards—one side of a square of same perimeter as outer
face of Sarsen Circle
> 276 remens—diameter of outer face of Inner Bank
> 27,600,000 furlongs—perimeter of a square drawn on the
> circumference of sun

The gematria for the titles of Jesus can be found in other places at Stonehenge, though they are most prominent in the Sarsen Circle. It is not surprising to find his numbers elsewhere in the monument for the interrelationship of the geometry of the circles is remarkable. Surely those circles were planned by one who not only understood the correlation of numbers, but who also took delight in it.

As mentioned above, the title "The Rabbi," whose number is 185, is found in the Sarsen Circle; however, if we omit the definite article, the title Rabbi, $\rho\alpha\beta\beta\iota$, is 115. The short side of the Station Stone rectangle is 115 feet while the radius of the Bluestone Horseshoe is 11.5 royal cubits. Jesus said *"I am the door,"* $\epsilon\lambda\omega\ \epsilon\iota\mu\iota\ \eta\ \theta\upsilon\rho\alpha$, which by gematria becomes 1391. There are .0001391 square miles in the area of a square whose perimeter equals the circumference of the Bluestone Circle. Jesus also said *"I am the way, the truth and the life,"* $\epsilon\gamma\omega\ \epsilon\iota\mu\iota\ \eta\ o\delta os\ \kappa\alpha\iota\ \eta\ \alpha\lambda\eta\theta\epsilon\iota\alpha\ \kappa\alpha\iota\ \eta\ \zeta\omega\eta$, 2182. There are .02182 furlongs in the radius of the Aubrey Circle and .2182 miles in the perimeter of a square drawn on the Aubrey Circle. He was also called the Word of God, translated from the Greek word *Logos,* $\lambda o\gamma os$, 373. There are 373 inches in one side of a square whose perimeter is the same as the circumference of the Bluestone Horseshoe.

115 = Rabbi, $\rho\alpha\beta\beta\iota$
115 feet—short side of Station Stone rectangle
11.5 royal cubits—radius of Bluestone Horseshoe

1391 = I am the door, εγω ειμι η θυρα
.0001391 square miles—area of a square of same perimeter
as Bluestone Circle

2182 = I am the Way, the Truth and the Life,
εγω ειμι η οδος και η αληθεια και η ζωη
.02182 furlongs—radius of the Aubrey Circle
.2182 miles—perimeter of a square drawn on the
Aubrey Circle

373 = Word (*Logos*), λογος
373 inches—one side of a square of same perimeter as
Bluestone Horseshoe

The number of those who will be associated with the Lamb
of God on Mount Zion is 144,000 (Revelation 7:4). When the
mean circumference of the Sarsen Circle is taken as the perimeter of a square, the area of that square is .0144 square
furlongs or .144 acres. These 144,000 are made up of those
who *"follow the Lamb withersoever he goeth"* (Revelation
14:4), *i.e.,* Christians. The number 144 is prominent at Stonehenge, as shown below.

144,000—number of those with the Lamb on Mount Zion
.0144 miles—one side of a square of the same perimeter as
inner face of Sarsen Circle
.0144 square furlongs—area of a square of same perimeter
as mean Sarsen Circle
.144 acres—area of a square of same perimeter as mean
Sarsen Circle
144 feet—radius of Aubrey Circle
144 Palestinian cubits—diameter of inner face of Inner Bank
1.44 furlongs—circumference of inner face of Inner Bank
144 royal cubits—circumference of Bluestone Circle
.0144 square furlongs—area of a square drawn on Bluestone
Circle
.144 acres—area of a square drawn on Bluestone Circle
.144 miles—perimeter of Station Stone rectangle

Jesus referred to this little group of his followers by using another number—153—the number of fish in the net (John 21: 11). This number is also prominent at Stonehenge.

153—number of fish in the net
.153 furlongs—mean diameter of Sarsen Circle
153 royal cubits—one side of a square drawn on outer face of Inner Bank
153 royal cubits—long side of Station Stone rectangle
15300 (15264) inches—perimeter of a square drawn on crest of Inner Bank
15300 (15271.7) square MY—area of a square drawn on outer face of Inner Bank

The relationship of the Heel Stone to the Sarsen Circle is shown by its distance as well as its tilt. It bows toward the monument at an angle of 30.° From the Sarsen Center to the base of the Heel Stone, as given by both Atkinson and Stone, is 256 feet. The gematria for Truth, $\alpha\lambda\eta\theta\eta s$, is 256. From the Sarsen Center to the approximate center of the Heel stone is roughly 258 feet, which can be divided into five units of 30 royal cubits each. For a measurement of this magnitude we use the royal cubit carried out to seven decimal places which gives the accuracy needed, *i.e.,* 1.7203907 feet. Thus 30 x 1.7203907 = 51.61172 feet per unit. The square of this number (51.61172^2) is 2664, or three times the number of Jesus (3 x 888 = 2664). With the addition of one unit it becomes the number of God the Father Almighty, $\Theta\epsilon os\ o\ \pi\alpha\tau\eta\rho\ \pi\alpha\nu\tauo$-$\kappa\rho\alpha\tau\omega\rho$, 2665.

The number 51.6 which connects the Sarsen Circle with the Heel Stone also relates to Israel's ancient Tabernacle, as does the number 888. Dimensions for the Tabernacle as given in the Hebrew Scriptures are in royal cubits. The tent-like structure was composed of two rooms called the Holy and the Most Holy (Holy of Holies). Their combined dimensions were 30 royal cubits long by 10 royal cubits wide, or 51.6 feet by 17.2

feet.* The area thus formed was 888 square feet. Surrounding the Tabernacle was the Court, enclosed with a white linen curtain. The perimeter of the Court was 516 feet or 300 royal cubits. As noted above, the title *"The Master"* is 586, however when we omit the definite article it becomes Master, διδασκαλος, 516.

516 = Master, διδασκαλος
51.6 feet—each of 5 units of 30 royal cubits each in distance from Sarsen Center to center of Heel Stone
516 feet—perimeter of Court of Tabernacle
51.6 feet—long side of Tabernacle (Holy and Most Holy)

888 = Jesus, 'Ιησους
888 square yards = area of mean of Sarsen Circle
888 square feet—area of Tabernacle (Holy and Most Holy)
.00888 square furlongs—area of a square of same perimeter as Bluestone Circle
.0888 acres—area of a square of same perimeter as Bluestone Circle

Other number relationships between the Sarsen Circle and Israel's Tabernacle are as follows:

260 remens—circumference of mean Sarsen Circle
.026 furlongs—short side of Tabernacle
.26 furlongs—long side of Court of Tabernacle
.026 miles—perimeter of Tabernacle
.026 furlongs—each side of Most Holy of Tabernacle
    .26 square furlongs—area of a square drawn on outer face of Inner Bank
    260 remens—perimeter of a square drawn on Bluestone Circle

*Some have used 18 inches for the cubit of the Tabernacle. There is no ancient cubit measuring 18 inches. The nearest would be the Babylonian cubit known as the moderate cubit—18.14 inches—which did not appear in Holy Scripture until about 1,000 years later, at the time of Ezekiel's vision. The author feels that the royal cubit was used in the building of the Tabernacle because of its beautiful geometrical harmony with Stonehenge, the Great Pyramid and the universe.

137 Roman paces—circumference of outer face of Sarsen
  Circle
1374 square MY—area of a square drawn on mean Sarsen
  Circle
137 feet—perimeter of Tabernacle
    137 Palestinian cubits—diameter of Aubrey Circle
    1.37 furlongs—circumference of Aubrey Circle
    .00137 MMi—radius of Bluestone Horseshoe
    137 square yards—area of Bluestone Horseshoe
    137 Palestinian cubits—diagonal of Station Stone
      rectangle

1060 square Roman paces—area of a square of same
  perimeter as mean Sarsen Circle
.0000106 square furlongs—area of Most Holy of Tabernacle
    106 MY—diameter of Aubrey Circle
    106 yards—diameter of crest of Inner Bank
    106 MY—diagonal of Station Stone rectangle
    1060 square Roman paces—area of a square drawn on
      Bluestone Circle

48 royal cubits—one side of a square of same perimeter as
  outer face of Sarsen Circle
48 Palestinian cubits—diameter of mean Sarsen Circle
.48 furlongs—circumference of mean Sarsen Circle
4807 inches—perimeter of a square drawn on mean
  Sarsen Circle
.0048 MMi—perimeter of Most Holy of Tabernacle
    48 yards—radius of Aubrey Circle
    .48 furlongs—perimeter of a square drawn on Bluestone
      Circle

.080 furlongs—radius of outer face of Sarsen Circle
80 royal cubits—perimeter of Tabernacle
    .080 MMi—perimeter of a square drawn on Aubrey
      Circle

32.5 Roman paces—one side of a square of same perimeter
as mean Sarsen Circle
.00325 miles—short side of Tabernacle
.00325 miles—each side of Most Holy of Tabernacle
    32.5 remens—diameter of Bluestone Horseshoe
    32.5 remens—radius of Bluestone Circle
    32.5 Roman paces—diameter of Bluestone Circle

.060 miles—circumference of mean Sarsen Circle
60 royal cubits—perimeter of Holy of Tabernacle
.0060 MMi—short side of Court of Tabernacle
    .060 furlongs—diameter of Bluestone Horseshoe
    .060 furlongs—radius of Bluestone Circle
    .060 miles—perimeter of a square drawn on Bluestone
        Circle
    .060 miles—diameter of crest of Inner Bank

.0000030 square MMi—area of inner face of Sarsen Circle
.000030 square MMi—area of a square of same perimeter as
mean Sarsen Circle
30 royal cubits—long side of Tabernacle
300 square royal cubits—area of Tabernacle
    .000030 square MMi—area of a square drawn on
        Bluestone Circle
    .030 miles—perimeter of a square drawn on Bluestone
        Horseshoe
    .030 miles—radius of crest of Inner Bank

.003396 square miles—area of a square drawn on inner face
of Sarsen Circle
.03396 square furlongs—area of Court of Tabernacle

STONEHENGE...A CLOSER LOOK

4240 (4238.64) square remens—area of a square of same
perimeter as mean Sarsen Circle
424 remens—perimeter of Court of Tabernacle
42.4 remens—long side of Tabernacle
    424 MY—perimeter of a square drawn on Aubrey Circle
    424 yards—perimeter of a square drawn on crest of
       Inner Bank
    4240 (4238.64) square remens—area of a square drawn
       on Bluestone Circle

28 MY—one side of a square of same perimeter as inner face
of Sarsen Circle
.028 MMi—perimeter of a square drawn on the mean Sarsen
Circle
.0000028 square MMi—area of Holy of Tabernacle

143 MY—perimeter of a square drawn on inner face of
Sarsen Circle
.00000143 square MMi—area of Most Holy of Tabernacle

130 yards—perimeter of a square drawn on inner face of
Sarsen Circle
130 Roman paces—circumference of mean Sarsen Circle
.130 furlongs—short side of Court of Tabernacle
.0130 miles—perimeter of Most Holy of Tabernacle
    .130 square furlongs—area of a square drawn on inner
       face of Inner Bank
    1.30 acres—area of a square drawn on inner face of
       Inner Bank
    130 Roman paces—perimeter of a square drawn on
       Bluestone Circle

.02122 MMi—circumference of inner face of Sarsen Circle
.00002122 square miles—area of Holy of Tabernacle

19.995 Roman paces—one side of a square drawn on inner
   face of Sarsen Circle
1999.5 square MY—area of Court of Tabernacle

39.99 remens—radius of inner face of Sarsen Circle
39.99 Roman paces—diameter of inner face of Sarsen Circle
39.98 square MY—area of Most Holy of Tabernacle
399.8 square remens—area of Holy of Tabernacle
   .3999 furlongs—one side of a square of same perimeter
      as outer face of Inner Bank

.120 furlongs—one side of a square of same perimeter as
   mean Sarsen Circle
120 square MY—area of Tabernacle
.120 MMi—short side of Tabernacle
.120 MMi—each side of Most Holy of Tabernacle
   .12 furlongs—diameter of Bluestone Circle
   12,000 (11994) square MY—area of outer face of
      Inner Bank
   12,000 (11988) inches—circumference of crest of
      Inner Bank

The Sarsen Circle and the Cosmos

The geometry of Stonehenge and the geometry of the cosmos bear a remarkable similarity. The dimensions of the
earth, sun and moon were obviously known to the builder.
Just as the risings and settings of the sun and moon marked
the chronology of man with precision, so the geometry of the
sun and moon and the geometry of Stonehenge belong to one
harmonious plan.

The mean circumference of the Sarsen Circle, 316.8 feet,
is a number clearly identified with the earth, sun and moon.
The diameter of the earth is 7920 miles and a square drawn on
a circle of that diameter has a perimeter of 31,680 miles. The
radius of the earth is 31,680 furlongs. The sun has a diameter
of 864,000 miles which is equal to 316,800 MMi (14,400 feet

107

=1 megalithic mile or 2.727272 miles=1 megalithic mile). The diameter of the moon is 2160 miles, and a square drawn on a circle of that diameter has a perimeter of 3168 MMi (8640 miles). The relationship of the Sarsen Circle to the moon is further demonstrated by its area. The radius of the moon is 1080 miles and the area of the Sarsen Circle is 1080 square MY. A square drawn on the inner diameter of the Sarsen Circle has an area of .02160 square furlongs.

If the circumference of the Sarsen Circle were taken as the perimeter of a square, a circle inscribed within that square would have the diameter of 79.2 feet, and this is found to be the extreme diameter of the Bluestone Circle. (See Figure 23.) The diameter of the moon is 2160 miles or 792.0 MMi, showing its relationship to the Bluestone Circle also. This corresponds to the earth which has a diameter of 7920 miles. Within the Bluestone Circle stands the Trilithon Horseshoe and within this magnificent structure stands the Bluestone Horseshoe. The stones of its closed side stand tangent to a circle with a diameter of 39.60 feet, which equals the radius of the Bluestone Circle. Thus the diameter of the Bluestone Horseshoe corresponds to the radius of the earth which is 3960 miles, and the radius of the moon, which is 396.0 MMi.

316.8 feet—circumference of mean Sarsen Circle
316,800 MMi—diameter of sun
31,680 furlongs—radius of earth
31,680 miles—perimeter of a square drawn on circumference of earth
3168 MMi—perimeter of a square drawn on circumference of moon

79.2 feet—diameter of Bluestone Circle
7920 miles—diameter of earth
792.0 MMi—diameter of moon

1080 square MY—area of mean Sarsen Circle
1080 miles—radius of moon

.02160 square furlongs—area of a square drawn on inner face
   of Sarsen Circle
.2160 acres—area of a square drawn on inner face of Sarsen
   Circle
2160 miles—diameter of moon

39.6 feet—diameter of Bluestone Horseshoe
39.6 feet—radius of Bluestone Circle
3960 miles—radius of earth
396.0 MMi—radius of moon

3456 inches—diameter of Aubrey Circle
3456 inches—diagonal of Station Stone rectangle
3,456,000 furlongs—radius of sun
3,456,000 miles—perimeter of a square drawn on
   circumference of sun

8641 square Roman paces—area of a square of same
   perimeter as Aubrey Circle
.00864 MMi—circumference of Bluestone Horseshoe
864,000 miles—diameter of sun
8640 furlongs—radius of moon
8640 miles—perimeter of a square drawn on
   circumference of moon

1728 inches—radius of Aubrey Circle
.01728 MMi—circumference of Bluestone Circle
17280 furlongs—diameter of moon

696.96 square yards—area of a square of same perimeter as
   mean Sarsen Circle
696.96 square yards—area of a square drawn on Bluestone
   Circle
69,696 square feet—area of a square of same perimeter as
   outer face of Inner Bank
6,969,600 yards—radius of earth

1267.2 inches—diameter of outer face of Sarsen Circle
12,672 inches—circumference of outer face of Inner Bank
1,267,200 MMi—perimeter of a square drawn on
   circumference of sun
12,672 = 4 x 3168

.0432 MMi—one side of a square of same perimeter as
   Bluestone Circle
432,000 miles—radius of sun

248.8139 feet—circumference of Bluestone Circle
248,813.9 MMi—one side of a square of same perimeter as
   circumference of sun
24,881.39 miles—circumference of earth
2,488.139 MMi—circumference of moon

62.20 feet—one side of a square of same perimeter as
   Bluestone Circle
6220 miles—one side of a square of same perimeter as
   circumference of earth
622.0 MMi—one side of a square of same perimeter as
   circumference of moon

The Sarsen Circle and the Great Pyramid

The Great Pyramid, as originally built, was a beautiful white jewel in the noonday sunshine. Its dazzling white casing stones captured and reflected the sun's rays and inspired the ancient Strabo to write that it was "like a building let down from heaven, untouched by human hands."

This magnificent structure, which still stands as a silent memorial to the wisdom and understanding of its builder was, however, incomplete from its beginning. The most ancient writers who have described it all tell us that it was without its very crown—the topstone. The builder had left the world's masterpiece uncrowned, as it were. Diodorus Siculus, the ancient classical writer, visited the Pyramid many centuries before it was looted by the Arabs and wrote that it was "entire and without the least decay," and that it tapered upward to a small square summit. (Diod. Sic. I, 63.4)

The missing topstone was not, however, the only seeming deficiency in the structure. The most conspicuous eccentricity is the position of the entrance. To the observer, facing the front of the Pyramid, *i.e.,* its northern face, the whole building appears to be somehow out of symmetry, giving it a look of imbalance and distortion. Had the builder made a mistake? Is it even thinkable that the master builder who designed that mathematical marvel would make such an obvious error as to place the entrance off center? If it were even off center a few inches we would wonder why, but it stands to the left of center an alarming and uncomfortable 286.1 Pyramid inches which is equal to about 24 feet.

Since all the interior passages and chambers were built in the same vertical north-south plane as the entrance, it follows that the entire passage system of the monument is displaced eastward 286.1 Pyramid inches. The Belgian astronomer, Professor Charles Lagrange of the Royal Observatory, Brussels, named this displacement *Le Déplacement Caractéristique* (The Displacement Factor).

In 1864-65 Professor C. Piazzi Smyth took measurements of the Great Pyramid. On the basis of those measurements he was able to extrapolate the valuable fact that π (3.14159) and y (365.242) constitute the basis of the Pyramid's geometric construction, the value of y being the number of days in the solar tropical year. At the time of this great undertaking, the base of the building was buried under huge piles of sand and stones. Therefore on the constructural basis of π and y, Professor Smyth concluded that the side length of the square base would be y Pyramid cubits. (25 Pyramid inches = 1 Pyramid cubit.) Thus the length of each side at its socket level base would equal the number of days in the solar tropical year.

Years later, after the debris was cleared away, modern surveys were undertaken and an accurate measurement could be obtained. The results were startling! They uncovered rectangular sockets beneath each of the four corners, and found that the building had been actually constructed some-what short of its original design. The survey showed that the original full design had been that the base length (at socket level) should have been 9131.05 Pyramid inches, but was actually constructed to measure 9059.525 Pyramid inches. The full design was found to be precisely as Professor Smyth had reasoned, *i.e.,* the side length was designed to be 365.242 Pyramid cubits. And as if this discovery were not enough to thrill any Pyramidologist, it was found that the difference between the full design and the actual construction was 286.1 Pyramid inches—the Displacement Factor. The shortening of the base by the builder had been no mistake! It was careful, intelligent design.

This obvious deficiency in the construction of the monu-ment would seem to suggest that the builder would, elsewhere in the structure, rectify or make it right. Since the Displace-ment Factor is a negative dimension of 286.1 Pyramid inches, an effective rectifying would require a plus dimension of 286.1 Pyramid inches. The rectifying of the displacement of the passage system should be found in the passage system, and the rectifying of the displacement of the exterior should be found somewhere in the exterior design; and so it is.

The rectification in the passage system was found to be in the height of the Grand Gallery. The two ascending passages, named First Ascending Passage and Grand Gallery, share the same floor line; however upon reaching the uppermost ex-tremity of the First Ascending Passage and stepping into the spacious darkness of the Grand Gallery, we find the roof suddenly to be 286.1 Pyramid inches higher. This grand ex-pansion of height is directly above the Christ Triangle. (For a description of the Christ Triangle please see Chapter 3.) Nowhere in its 286.1 Pyramid inches is to be found any eccen-tricity, deficiency, imperfection nor contraction but just the opposite of these. It is 286.1 Pyramid inches of uplift, expan-sion and enlargement. It was found to be a factor of equal dimension but with an opposite function to the Displacement Factor; therefore it has been named the Rectification Factor.

That this Rectification Factor appears directly over the

geometric illustration of the death and resurrection of Jesus, in 33 A.D., provides the fitting illustration of the value of his sacrificed life—it rectifies that which had been displaced by Adamic sin. The Apostle Paul expressed it thus:

"For since by man (Adam) came death, by man (Jesus) came also the resurrection of the dead." I Corinthians 15:21

The Rectification Factor of the Great Pyramid reveals that the mighty power of the resurrected Jesus is the one great and only power adequate to rectify dying mankind and bring them to ultimate restitution. The Rectification Factor as found in the exterior design serves to verify and amplify this truth.

This beautiful white Pyramid was left without its crowning topstone. The topstone of a pyramid is the only stone in the structure which is itself a perfect pryamid, thus the topstone serves as a model for the whole building. The topstone for the Great Pyramid would have been enormous in size. Each side would have a length of 572.2 Pyramid inches (2 times the Rectification Factor). This would be nearly 48 feet, while the height would have been 30 feet. As a single stone, it would have been colossal! No wonder it was never lifted into place! Had it, however, been somehow lifted and placed into position, its perimeter would have overhung the summit platform by a circuit of 286.1 Pyramid inches. This is due to the displacement of the base of the structure from its original full design. Thus the 286.1 Pyramid inches by which the topstone would overhang exactly rectifies the 286.1 Pyramid inches in the displacement of the base of the monument. The base perimeter of the topstone would be 2288.8 Pyramid inches, which is precisely 8 times the Rectification Factor (8 x 286.1 = 2288.8). The gematria for Christ the Lord, Χριστος Κυριος, is 2288 and 8 is the number used in the symbology of the Scriptures to represent the resurrection.

That this colossal mass of rock—this perfect topstone—should represent Jesus is referred to in both the Hebrew and Greek Scriptures.

"The stone which the builders refused is become the head-

stone of the corner, this is the Lord's doing; it is marvelous in our eyes." Psalm 118:22, 23

"He shall bring forth the headstone thereof with shoutings, crying, Grace, grace unto it." Zechariah 4:7

"Therefore thus saith the Lord God, Behold, I lay in Zion for a foundation a stone, a tried stone, a precious corner-stone, a sure foundation." Isaiah 28:16

"Be it known unto you all, and to all the people of Israel, that by the name of Jesus Christ of Nazareth, whom ye crucified, whom God raised from the dead, even by him doth this man stand here before you whole. This is the stone which was set at nought of you builders, which is become the head of the corner. Neither is there salvation in any other: for there is none other name under heaven given among men, whereby we must be saved." Acts 4:10-12

"...and are built upon the foundation of the apostles and prophets, Jesus Christ himself being the chief corner stone." Ephesians 2:20

"Wherefore also it is contained in the scripture, Behold, I lay in Zion a chief corner stone, elect, precious: and he that believeth on him shall not be confounded. Unto you therefore which believe he is precious: but unto them which be disobedient, the stone which the builders disallowed, the same is made the head of the corner." I Peter 2:6, 7

From the foregoing evidence contained in this chapter it is not with timidity that we suggest that the Sarsen Circle of Stonehenge relates to Jesus. Thus it seems fitting that we should look for the Great Pyramid's Rectification Factor in its geometry. We do not have to look far. The area of the mean of the Sarsen Circle is .002861 square miles. This was obviously not by chance, but was designed to show the beautiful harmony between these two magnificent monuments— a harmony of design which points unmistakably to Jesus.

If the Rectification Factor were expressed in terms of the Megalithic Mile instead of Pyramid inches it would measure .001657 MMi. And we find that the perimeter of a square drawn on the mean of the Sarsen Circle measures 165.7 Roman paces. The Rectification Factor, which is so important in the geometry of the Great Pyramid, is thus confirmed as relating to Jesus by the geometry of the Sarsen Circle.

In Isaiah 28:16 this beautiful perfect topstone is called *"a tried stone, a precious corner stone,"* בחן אבן יקר פנה אבן, which is 611. How appropriate to find that the perimeter of a square drawn on the mean of the Sarsen Circle measures .611 furlongs.

Further evidence that the perfect topstone represents Jesus can be found in the gematria for another name by which he is known in the Greek Scriptures, *i.e.,* Advocate, παρακλητος, 810. The base diagonal of the topstone is 810 inches.

If the Great Pyramid's form were perfected and brought into conformity to the topstone, all the four sides must be filled out with masonry until they have come into exact alignment with the angles of the projecting perfect topstone. The result would be that the square base of the monument would be enlarged by 286.1 Pyramid inches, bringing the four corners to the full measure of the sockets. With this rectification complete and in perfect alignment with the topstone, the perimeter of the base would measure 365.242 Pyramid cubits, or the number of days in the solar tropical year. But it would do something else too! It would result in the fact that each side of the base would measure .144 miles. The number 144, as has been shown, is a tremendously significant number at Stonehenge. The area of a square of the same perimeter as the mean of the Sarsen Circle is .0144 square furlongs or .144 acres. One side of a square of the same perimeter as the inner face of the Sarsen Circle is .0144 miles. It is also noteworthy that one side of the base of the Pyramid if rectified out to its full design would measure 280 MY and there are .0280 MMi in the perimeter of a square drawn on the mean of the Sarsen Circle.

The length of one side of the base of the Pyramid when rectified out to its full original design is nearly identical to the perimeter of the Station Stone rectangle at Stonehenge. The difference for a measurement of this magnitude would be considered insignificant were it not for the astonishing fact that this difference is precisely 3.52 feet. As has been shown, the average interval between the uprights of the Sarsen Circle is 3.52 feet. The lintels which top the uprights can be divided into thirds, *i.e.,* one third rests on half an upright, one third spans the gap, and one third rests on the next upright. Thus each third measures 3.52 feet and each half an upright measures 3.52 feet. The diameter of the outer face of the Sarsen Circle is 3.52 yards and, as has been shown, the name by which Jesus referred to himself, The Way, η οδος is 352. If one side of the Pyramid differs from the perimeter of the Station Stone rectangle by 3.52 feet, then the entire base of the Pyramid differs from four times the Station Stone rectangle by 14.08 feet (4 x 3.52 = 14.08). The gematria for Savior, σωτηρ, is 1408 and 140.8 yards is the perimeter of a square drawn on the outer face of the Sarsen Circle. Who can deny that the Sarsen Circle and the Great Pyramid relate to Jesus!

Within the Great Pyramid there are two chambers above ground level, called the King's Chamber and Queen's Chamber. The geometry of these two rooms bears a remarkable relationship to the Sarsen Circle as shown below.

1167 inches—diameter of inner face of Sarsen Circle
.00001167 square miles—area of Queen's Chamber floor
   .01167 MMi—radius of outer face of Inner Bank

32.55 Roman paces—one side of a square of same perimeter
   as mean Sarsen Circle
.0032557 miles—width of King's Chamber
.0032557 miles—width of Queen's Chamber
   .003257 miles—short side of Tabernacle (Holy and
     Most Holy)
   .003257 miles—each side of Most Holy
   32.55 remens—diameter of Bluestone Horseshoe
   32.55 remens—radius of Bluestone Circle
   32.55 Roman paces—diameter of Bluestone Circle

260 remens—circumference of mean Sarsen Circle
.0260 furlongs—width of King's Chamber
.0260 furlongs—width of Queen's Chamber
26 royal cubits—length of King's Chamber complex (Great
    Step to far side of King's Chamber)
    .0260 furlongs—short side of Tabernacle (Holy and
      Most Holy)
    .260 furlongs—long side of Court of Tabernacle
    .0260 miles—perimeter of Tabernacle
    .0260 furlongs—each side of Most Holy
    .26 square furlongs—area of a square drawn on outer
      face of Inner Bank

256 feet—distance from Sarsen Center to base of Heel Stone
.0256 square furlongs—area of a square drawn on outer face
  of Sarsen Circle
.256 acres—area of a square drawn on outer face of Sarsen
  Circle
25.6 feet—diagonal of Queen's Chamber floor
    256 = Truth,
    .0000256 square MMi—area of Bluestone Circle
    25.6 remens—one side of a square of same perimeter as
      Bluestone Horseshoe
    25.6 Roman paces—one side of a square of same
      perimeter as Bluestone Circle

148.8 royal cubits—distance from Sarsen Center to base of
  Heel Stone
.001488 MMi—perimeter of Coffer in King's Chamber

.0002861 square miles—area of mean Sarsen Circle
286.1 Pyramid inches—Displacement and Rectification
  Factor of Pyramid

165.7 Roman paces—perimeter of a square drawn on mean
  Sarsen Circle
.001657 MMi—Displacement and Rectification Factor of
  Pyramid

STONEHENGE...A CLOSER LOOK

.0280 MMi—perimeter of a square drawn on mean Sarsen
   Circle
280 MY—one side of Pyramid base (full design)

.0144 miles—one side of a square of same perimeter as inner
   face of Sarsen Circle
.0144 square furlongs—area of a square of same perimeter as
   mean Sarsen Circle
.144 acres—area of a square of same perimeter as mean
   Sarsen Circle
.144 miles—one side of Pyramid base (full design)
   144 feet—radius of Aubrey Circle
   144 Palestinian cubits—diameter of inner face of
      Inner Bank
   1.44 furlongs—circumference of inner face of
      Inner Bank
   144 royal cubits—circumference of Bluestone Circle
   .0144 square furlongs—area of a square drawn on
      Bluestone Circle
   .144 acres—area of a square drawn on Bluestone Circle
   .144 miles—perimeter of Station Stone rectangle

.153 furlongs—diameter of mean Sarsen Circle
1.53 Palestinian cubits—width of Coffer in King's Chamber
153 Pyramid inches x 12 = length of roof of Grand Gallery
153 Pyramid inches—length of entrance passages to King's
   Chamber
   153—number of fish in the net
   153 royal cubits—one side of a square drawn on outer
      face of Inner Bank
   153 royal cubits—long side of Station Stone rectangle

56.6 royal cubits—diameter of inner face of Sarsen Circle
.000566 MMi—diagonal of Coffer in King's Chamber (floor)

79.9 remens—diameter of inner face of Sarsen Circle
79.9 square MY—area of King's Chamber floor

118

1413 square Palestinian cubits—area of a square of same
   perimeter as mean Sarsen Circle
14.13 remens—width of King's Chamber
14.13 remens—width of Queen's Chamber
14.13 MY—diagonal of King's Chamber floor

28.3 royal cubits—radius of inner face of Sarsen Circle
28.3 remens—length of King's Chamber

2288.8 Pyramid inches—perimeter of topstone base
2288 = Christ the Lord, Χριστος Κυριος

.611 furlongs—perimeter of a square drawn on mean
   Sarsen Circle
611 = *"a tried stone, a precious corner stone"*

810 inches—diagonal of topstone base
810 = Advocate, παρακλητος

3.52 feet—difference between one side of Pyramid base and
   Station Stone rectangle
352 = The Way, η οδος
3.52 feet—average interval between Sarsen uprights
35.2 yards—diameter of outer face of Sarsen Circle
   352 yards—circumference of outer face of Inner Bank

14.08 feet—difference between Pyramid base and 4 times the
   Station Stone rectangle
1408 = Saviour, σωτηρ
140.8 yards—perimeter of a square drawn on outer face of
   Sarsen Circle
14.08 = 4 x 3.52

STONEHENGE...A CLOSER LOOK

Other relationships to the Sarsen Circle

The number 3168, Lord Jesus Christ, Κυριος 'Ιησους Χριστος, is the most prominent number in the geometry of Stonehenge. The mean circumference of the Sarsen Circle is 316.8 feet, and the relationship of this to the other circles of the monument is awesome. The repetition of other numbers is equally impressive. The extreme diameter of the Inner Bank is 336.135 feet, giving a circumference of 1056 feet or 352 yards. The length of the lintels of the Sarsen Circle is 10.56 feet and the intervals between the uprights is 3.52 feet. The extreme diameter of the Sarsen Circle is 105.6 feet or 35.2 yards. These numbers bear a relationship to 316.8 in that 3 x 35.2 = 105.6 and 3 x 105.6 = 316.8. The mean circumference of the Sarsen Circle is 105.6 yards while the perimeter of a square drawn on the Bluestone Circle is also 105.6 yards. The number 79.2, which is the diameter of the Bluestone Circle, also bears a relationship to 316.8 because 79.2 x 4 = 316.8. There are 31680 feet in six miles.

3168 = Lord Jesus Christ, Κυριος 'Ιησους Χριστος
316.8 feet—circumference of mean Sarsen Circle
316.8 feet—perimeter of a square drawn on Bluestone Circle
316.8 yards—circumference of inner face of Inner Bank
3168 inches—one side of a square of same perimeter as outer face of Inner Bank
3168 inches—long side of Station Stone rectangle
3168 = 3 x 1056
3168 = 4 x 792

352 = The Way, η οδος
35.2 yards—diameter of outer face of Sarsen Circle
3.52 feet—average interval between Sarsen uprights
352 yards—circumference of outer face of Inner Bank

1056 = 3 x 352
1056 = 4 x 264 (The Truth)
1056 = 1/5 mile

10.56 feet—length of each Sarsen lintel
105.6 feet—diameter of outer face of Sarsen Circle
105.6 yards—circumference of mean Sarsen Circle
105.6 yards—perimeter of a square drawn on Bluestone Circle
1056 feet—circumference of outer face of Inner Bank

264 = The Truth, $\eta\ \alpha\lambda\eta\theta\eta s$
26.4 yards—one side of a square of same perimeter as mean
    Sarsen Circle
264 feet—one side of a square of same perimeter as outer
    face of Inner Bank
264 feet—long side of Station Stone rectangle
26.4 yards—diameter of Bluestone Circle
264 = 792 ÷ 3
264 = 1056 ÷ 4

79.2 feet—one side of a square of same perimeter as mean
    Sarsen Circle
79.2 feet—diameter of Bluestone Circle
79.2 yards—one side of a square of same perimeter as inner
    face of Inner Bank

    All of the circles of Stonehenge bear interesting relationships to the Sarsen Circle. This amazing circle of 30 stones which clearly represents Jesus was, as it were, a pattern for the geometry of the whole structure. Some of these relationships are listed below.

    Due to the present condition of the site, the Inner Bank and Ditch which surround the monument do not lend themselves to precise measurement. Different authors give different figures, but all within reasonable proximity. The dimensions used here for the Inner Bank are averages of the figures that are available. Their correlation with other established numbers of the monument lend weight to their correctness.

STONEHENGE...A CLOSER LOOK

1674 square Palestinian cubits—area of inner face of
   Sarsen Circle
167.4 royal cubits—diameter of Aubrey Circle
167.4 royal cubits—diagonal of Station Stone rectangle

52.8 feet—radius of outer face of Sarsen Circle
52.8 yards—perimeter of a square drawn on Bluestone
   Horseshoe

272.7 remens—circumference of outer face of Sarsen Circle
.02727 miles—diameter of Aubrey Circle

.0000302 square MMi—area of a square of same perimeter as
   mean Sarsen Circle
302 yards—circumference of Aubrey Circle
.0000302 square MMi—area of a square drawn on Bluestone
   Circle

.0628 miles—circumference of outer face of Sarsen Circle
62.8 remens—one side of a square of same perimeter as
   inner face of Sarsen Circle
.0628 MMi—circumference of Aubrey Circle

31.41 Roman paces—one side of a square of same perimeter
   as inner face of Sarsen Circle
.0003141 square miles—area of mean Sarsen Circle
.0003141 square MMi—area of Aubrey Circle

226 royal cubits—perimeter of a square drawn on inner face
   of Sarsen Circle
226 feet—one side of a square of same perimeter as
   Aubrey Circle

.589 furlongs—perimeter of a square drawn on inner face of
   Sarsen Circle
.00589 miles—one side of a square of same perimeter as
   Bluestone Horseshoe

174 Roman paces—perimeter of a square drawn on outer
  face of Sarsen Circle
.174 furlongs—short side of Station Stone rectangle
174 square yards—area of a square drawn on Bluestone
  Horseshoe

403.3 feet—perimeter of a square drawn on mean
  Sarsen Circle
4033 inches—diameter of outer face of Inner Bank

2291 square Palestinian cubits—area of a square drawn on
  mean Sarsen Circle
.2291 furlongs—radius of inner face of Inner Bank

.076393 miles—perimeter of a square drawn on mean
  Sarsen Circle
.076393 furlongs—radius of mean Sarsen Circle

134 yards—perimeter of a square drawn on mean Sarsen
  Circle
.0134 square furlongs—area of a square of same perimeter as
  inner face of Sarsen Circle
.134 acres—area of a square of same perimeter as inner face
  of Sarsen Circle
13413.81 square Roman paces—area of crest of Inner Bank

1129.86 square yards—area of a square drawn on mean
  Sarsen Circle
112986 square feet—area of a square drawn on outer face of
  Inner Bank

.1256 furlongs—one side of a square of same perimeter as
  outer face of Sarsen Circle
125.6 Roman paces—circumference of inner face of
  Sarsen Circle
1256 square Roman paces—area of inner face of Sarsen
  Circle

112.38 MY—circumference of inner face of Sarsen Circle

11236 square yards—area of a square drawn on crest of
Inner Bank

1674 square Palestinian cubits—area of inner face of
Sarsen Circle

167.4 royal cubits—diagonal of Station Stone rectangle

764.2 square yards—area of a square of same perimeter as
outer face of Sarsen Circle

76.42 feet—one side of a square drawn on inner face of
Sarsen Circle

36.3 Palestinian cubits—one side of a square of same
perimeter as inner face of Sarsen Circle

3630 inches—diameter of inner face of Inner Bank

.00363 square miles—area of a square drawn on crest of
Inner Bank

28.1 MY—one side of a square of same perimeter as inner
face of Sarsen Circle

.0000281 square MMi—area of a square of same perimeter as
inner face of Sarsen Circle

1167 inches—diameter of inner face of Sarsen Circle

.01167 MMi—radius of outer face of Inner Bank

.01842 miles—diameter of inner face of Sarsen Circle

184.2 royal cubits—circumference of mean Sarsen Circle

184.2 royal cubits—perimeter of a square drawn on
Bluestone Circle

50.42 feet—radius of mean Sarsen Circle

50.42 yards—diameter of inner face of Inner Bank

33.61 yards—diameter of mean Sarsen Circle
336.1 feet—diameter of outer face of Inner Bank
.0003361 square MMi—area of a square of same perimeter
  as outer face of Inner Bank

.0000383 square MMi—area of mean Sarsen Circle
.000383 square MMi—area of crest of Inner Bank
38.3 yards—short side of Station Stone rectangle

43.4 remens—circumference of outer face of Sarsen Circle
43.4 Roman paces—diameter of outer face of Sarsen Circle
434 Roman paces—circumference of outer face of Inner Bank

    The geometry of the Sarsen Circle is truly amazing! How
did the builder know the geometry of the earth, sun and
moon? How did he know the dimensions of Israel's Tabernacle which had not yet been built? Had he seen the Great
Pyramid; or had he an intimate acquaintance with its builder?
    The builder, whoever he was, had a remarkable knowledge
of geometry and its relationship to the gematria of the Bible.

photo by Thomas Gilbert

The beautiful symmetry of the Moonrise Trilithon has survived the ravages of time, tempest and tourists.

8

Stonehenge, The New Jerusalem and the Cosmos

"And the city lieth four-square, and the length is as large as the breadth: and he measured the city with the reed, twelve thousand furlongs. The length and breadth and the height of it are equal. And he measured the wall thereof, an hundred and forty and four cubits, according to the measure of a man, that is, of the angel." (Revelation 21:16, 17)

There is a remarkable correspondency between Stonehenge and the New Jerusalem. The dimensions of the stone circles of Stonehenge are numerically the same, though on a reduced scale, as those of the Apostle John's description of the New Jerusalem. The geometry of the ground plans of both are the same, but for one aspect: whereas the city takes the form of a square, Stonehenge is circular. The fact is, that the vision which the Apostle John was given on the Isle of Patmos, in 90 A.D., was prefigured 2,000 years earlier on that lonely plain in southern England, by the stark stone circles of Stonehenge.

How did the Apostle John know the dimensions of Stonehenge? Or did he? He wrote only what he saw in vision. No, John surely did not know! But the One who gave him the vision must have known. The only other conclusion would be that it is merely coincidence that the two ground plans should coincide. "Stonehenge" and "coincidence" do not even share the same world.

Stonehenge, by its geometry does, however, share the universe. And it shares the geometry of the New Jerusalem. It is not enough that we should ask if the Apostle John knew the dimensions of Stonehenge, for the real question is far more fundamental. Did the builder of Stonehenge have fore-knowledge of the prophetic New Jerusalem?

The description which John gave seems rather puzzling at first. A city as large as 12,000 furlongs per side (1,500 miles) would surely have a wall far greater than 144 cubits, for this is the measure of the small Bluestone Circle at Stonehenge. The two measurements seem not to be related. The problem is solved by the fact that what John was describing differs in scale but belongs to one geometric figure. When they are brought to commensurable proportions it is found that a square of 12 furlongs contains a circle of 14,400 cubits. But the New Jerusalem is not a square, but a cube—a cube containing a sphere. The sphere is in fact a model of the earth for its diameter is 7920 units and earth's mean diameter is 7920 miles. The cube is 1440 acres per side and when multiplied by its six sides gives a total measure of 8640 acres—864,000 miles being the diameter of the sun.

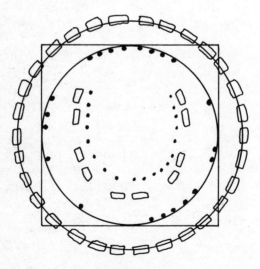

Figure 27

The ground plan, however, is commensurate with the ground plan of Stonehenge. The perimeter of the square of the New Jerusalem is 48,000 furlongs, or 31,680,000 feet. If this figure is reduced to 316.8 (the perimeter of the Sarsen Circle), and the square superimposed upon the circle, the circle within that square would form the exact dimensions of the outer circumference of the Bluestone Circle, *i.e.*, a circumference of 144 royal cubits, or 248 feet, giving a diameter of 79.2 feet.

As already noted, the Great Pyramid monumentalized the relationship of the circle to the square, for its outer angle of 51°51'14.3" is the π angle. The vertical height of the Pyramid bears the same ratio to its square base as the radius of a circle bears to its circumference. The perimeter of a circle can never be defined precisely because of the infinite nature of π. The square and circle are therefore incommensurable for there is no way of showing that the perimeter of a circle is exactly equal to that of a given square. It is evident that the geometry of Stonehenge and the New Jerusalem is the harmonizing of these two fundamental opposites. Stonehenge, like the New Jerusalem, is representative of the completed plan of God, the at-one-ment of two heretofore irreconcilable opposites, man and his Creator. The square and circle, as shown by the New Jerusalem, Stonehenge and the Great Pyramid monumentalize the whole objective of God's plan relative to man, *i.e.*, the reconciling of man to Himself in an everlasting union of oneness—the marriage of the circle and the square. The vision which the Apostle John saw conveyed to him the concept of a marriage.

> *"And I John saw the holy city, the New Jerusalem, coming down from God out of heaven, prepared as a bride adorned for her husband. And I heard a great voice out of heaven saying, Behold, the tabernacle of God is with men, and he will dwell with them, and they shall be his people, and God himself shall be with them, and be their God. And God shall wipe away all tears from their eyes; and there shall be no more death, neither sorrow, nor crying, neither shall there*

be any more pain; for the former things are passed away."
(Revelation 21:2-4)

John revealed to us the effect of this marriage, *i.e.,* oneness between man and his Creator, and everlasting life.

The correlation of the numbers of Stonehenge, the New Jerusalem and the cosmos are startling. An examination of these number relationships causes us once again to stand in awe of that marvelous old monument. How did the builder know the geometry of the universe?

The number 3168, Lord Jesus Christ, Κυριος 'Ιησους Χριστος, is the most prominent number of Stonehenge, therefore it is not surprising to find the perimeter of the New Jerusalem to be 31,680,000 feet.

The solar number 864 is also found in the New Jerusalem, for 864,000,000 square furlongs or 8640 acres is the sum of its six sides. The name Jerusalem, 'Ιερουσαλημ, is 864.

The number 144 has also been shown to be a prominent Stonehenge number. The spherical wall of the New Jerusalem has a circumference of 14,400,000 royal cubits, while the area of the cube which surrounds it is 1440 acres on each side.

The circumference drawn on the mean diameter of the earth is 24,881.3 miles. The circumference of the Bluestone Circle is 248.813 feet and the circumference of the moon is 2,488.13 MMi. If the circumference of the sun were taken as the perimeter of a square, one side of that square would be 248,813 MMi. If the area of the mean of the Sarsen Circle were squared, the perimeter of that square would be .0248 MMi.

The number 1056 is also interesting in its relationships. The length of those perfect lintels is 10.56 feet. The mean circumference of the Sarsen Circle is 105.60 yards, while the perimeter of a square drawn on the Bluestone circle is also 105.60 yards. The extreme diameter of the Sarsen Circle is 105.6 feet and the circumference of the outer face of the Inner Bank is 1056 feet. The perimeter of the New Jerusalem is 10,560,000 yards. The mystery of this number increases when we find that it is also used in Revelation 14:20. The treading of the winepress of the wrath of God causes blood to come out of the winepress by the space of 1,056,000 feet. Whatever it may mean, it is certainly a number commensurate with Stonehenge and the New Jerusalem. The table below shows these, as well as other relationships between Stonehenge, the New Jerusalem and the cosmos.

31,680,000 feet—perimeter of the New Jerusalem
3168 = Lord Jesus Christ, Κυριος Ιησους Χριστος
316.8 feet—circumference of mean Sarsen Circle
316.8 feet—perimeter of a square drawn on Bluestone Circle
316.8 yards—circumference of inner face of Inner Bank
3168 inches—one side of a square of same perimeter as
   outer face of Inner Bank
3168 inches—long side of Station Stone rectangle
316,800 MMi—diameter of sun
31,680 furlongs—radius of earth
31,680 miles—perimeter of a square drawn on circumference
   of earth
3,168 MMi—perimeter of a square drawn on circumference
   of moon
31,680 feet = 6 miles
316.8 = 3 x 105.6
316.8 = 4 x 79.2

864,000,000 square furlongs—sum of six sides of
   New Jerusalem
8640 acres—sum of six sides of New Jerusalem
864 = Jerusalem, Ἰερουσαλημ
864 = Holy of Holies, αγιων
864 = Saints, αγιων
864 = Corner stone, γωνια
864,000 miles—diameter of sun
8640 furlongs—radius of moon
8640 miles—perimeter of a square drawn on circumference
   of moon

STONEHENGE...A CLOSER LOOK

.00864 MMi—circumference of Bluestone Horseshoe
8641 square Roman paces—area of a square of same
  perimeter as Aubrey Circle
864,000 = 6 x 144,000

14,400,000 royal cubits—circumference of wall of
  New Jerusalem
144,000,000 square furlongs—one side of New Jerusalem
1440 acres—one side of New Jerusalem
.0144 square furlongs—area of a square of same perimeter as
  mean Sarsen Circle
.144 acres—area of a square of same perimeter as mean
  Sarsen Circle
144 feet—radius of Aubrey Circle
.0144 miles—one side of a square of same perimeter as inner
  face of Sarsen Circle
144 Palestinian cubits—diameter of inner face of Inner Bank
1.44 furlongs—circumference of inner face of Inner Bank
144 royal cubits—circumference of Bluestone Circle
.0144 square furlongs—area of a square drawn on Bluestone
  Circle
.144 acres—area of a square drawn on Bluestone Circle
.144 miles—perimeter of Station Stone rectangle
144,000—number of those with the Lamb on Mount Zion
14,400 feet—1 megalithic mile (MMi)

24,881,392 feet—circumference of wall of New Jerusalem
248.8139 feet—circumference of Bluestone Circle
24,881.39 miles—circumference of earth
248,813.9 MMi—one side of a square of same perimeter
  as sun
248,813.9 MMi—circumference of moon
.0248 MMi—perimeter of mean Sarsen Circle squared

264,000 yards—one side of New Jerusalem
264 = The Truth, $\eta\ \alpha\lambda\eta\theta\eta s$

132

26.4 yards—one side of a square of same perimeter as mean
  Sarsen Circle
264 square Roman paces—area of a square drawn on
  Bluestone Horseshoe
264 feet—one side of a square of same perimeter as outer
  face of Inner Bank
264 feet—long side of Station Stone rectangle
26.4 yards—diameter of Bluestone Circle
264 = 792 ÷ 3
264 = 1056 ÷ 4

1728 MMi—circumference of wall of New Jerusalem
1728,000,000,000 cubic furlongs—volume of New Jerusalem
17,280 furlongs—diameter of moon
.01728 MMi—circumference of Bluestone Circle
1728 inches—radius of Aubrey Circle

11,640,000 MY—perimeter of New Jerusalem
1164 = Son of God, $\nu\iota os\ \Theta\varepsilon o\nu$
116.4 MY—circumference of mean Sarsen Circle
116.4 MY—perimeter of a square drawn on Bluestone Circle

10,560,000 yards—perimeter of New Jerusalem
10.56 feet—length of each lintel
1056 feet—circumference of outer face of Inner Bank
105.6 feet—diameter of outer face of Sarsen Circle
105.6 yards—circumference of mean Sarsen Circle
105.6 yards—perimeter of a square drawn on Bluestone
  Circle
1056 feet = 1/5 mile
1056 = 3 x 352
1056 = 4 x 264
1,056,000 feet—Revelation 14:20: blood came out of the
  winepress

133

37,699 furlongs—circumference of wall of New Jerusalem
3,769.39 square royal cubits—area of a square drawn on
outer face of Sarsen Circle
.37699 furlongs—circumference of Bluestone Circle

8,293,797 yards—circumference of wall of New Jerusalem
82.94 feet—one side of a square of same perimeter as outer
face of Sarsen Circle
82.94 yards—circumference of Bluestone Circle
82,944 square feet—area of a square drawn on Aubrey Circle

6,969,600,000,000 square yards—area of one side of
New Jerusalem
6,969,600 yards—radius of earth
696.96 square yards—area of a square of same perimeter as
mean Sarsen Circle
696.96 square yards—area of a square drawn on Bluestone
Circle
69,696 square feet—area of a square of same perimeter as
outer face of Inner Bank

12,000 furlongs—one side of New Jerusalem
.12 (.1194) MMi—short side of Tabernacle (Holy and
Most Holy)
120 (119.9) square MY—area of Tabernacle (Holy and
Most Holy)
12,000 (11994) square MY—area of outer face of Inner Bank
12,000 (11988) inches—circumference of crest of Inner Bank
.12 furlongs—diameter of Bluestone Circle
.12 (.1199) furlongs—one side of a square of same perimeter
as mean Sarsen Circle

1,500 miles—one side of New Jerusalem

1500 = Mount Zion, $o\rho os\, \Sigma\iota\omega\nu$

150 Palestinian cubits—circumference of mean Sarsen Circle

.0150 miles—diameter of Bluestone Circle

150 Palestinian cubits—perimeter of a square drawn on Bluestone Circle

150 royal cubits—distance from Sarsen Center to center of Heel Stone

11,800,000 (11,808,819) Palestinian cubits—wall of New Jerusalem

.0118 square miles—area of a square of same perimeter as Bluestone Circle

118 Roman paces—diameter of Aubrey Circle

118 remens—radius of Aubrey Circle

118 Palestinian cubits—one side of a square of same perimeter as crest of Inner Bank

118 square MY—area of outer face of Sarsen Circle

118 Palestinian cubits—circumference of Bluestone Circle

48,000 furlongs—perimeter of New Jerusalem

.0048 MMi—perimeter of Most Holy of Tabernacle

.48 furlongs—perimeter of a square drawn on Bluestone Circle

48 royal cubits—one side of a square of same perimeter as outer face of Sarsen Circle

.48 furlongs—mean circumference of Sarsen Circle

48 Palestinian cubits—mean diameter of Sarsen Circle

48 yards—radius of Aubrey Circle

4807 inches—perimeter of a square drawn on mean Sarsen Circle

STONEHENGE...A CLOSER LOOK

302,500 square MMi—area of one side of New Jerusalem
302.5 feet—diameter of inner face of Inner Bank
.00003025 square MMi—area of a square of same perimeter
  as mean Sarsen Circle
.00003025 square MMi—area of a square drawn on
  Bluestone Circle

2,200 MMi—perimeter of New Jerusalem
.22 miles—short side of Station Stone rectangle
.0022 square furlongs—area of a square of same perimeter
  as Bluestone Horseshoe
.022 acres—area of a square of same perimeter as
  Bluestone Horseshoe
.022 MMi—circumference of mean Sarsen Circle
.022 MMi—diameter of crest of Inner Bank
.022 square miles—area of a square of same perimeter as
  crest of Inner Bank
.022 MMi—perimeter of a square drawn on Bluestone Circle
.00022 square miles—area of a square drawn on Bluestone
  Circle
.00022 square miles—area of a square of same perimeter as
  mean Sarsen Circle

3,456 square MMi—area of sphere of New Jerusalem
  (outer surface)
3,456 inches—diagonal of Station Stone rectangle
3,456,000 furlongs—radius of sun
3,456,000 miles—perimeter of a square drawn on
  circumference of sun

6,000 miles—perimeter of New Jerusalem
60 royal cubits—perimeter of Holy of Tabernacle
.006 MMi—short side of Court of Tabernacle
.06 miles—perimeter of a square drawn on Bluestone Circle
.06 furlongs—radius of Bluestone Circle
.06 miles—diameter of crest of Inner Bank

.06 miles—circumference of mean Sarsen Circle
.06 furlongs—diameter of Bluestone Horseshoe

The number 6

Following their exodus from Egyptian bondage, the Israelites, under the leadership of Moses, spent 40 years in the wilderness, wandering from place to place, enroute to their future homeland, Canaan, a portion of which is now the land of Israel. Prophetic time in the Hebrew Scriptures is based on the year of 360 days. Using this prophetic time method, Israel's 40 years enroute to Canaan would be $40 \times 360 = 14,400$ which symbolizes the number of those who will be with the Lamb on Mount Zion.

But when the Israelites reached the land of Canaan, they were confronted with the task of crossing the river Jordan. Their leader, Moses, had died, and Joshua was now to lead them across the flooded Jordan and into their promised land. As a memorial to this great event, for a people who had been homeless for forty years, Joshua instructed twelve men (one man from each tribe) to take a stone from the midst of the river and carry it to the other side. These twelve stones were then placed in a circle in Gilgal. The name Gilgal in the Hebrew language means circle. The gematria for Gilgal in Hebrew, גלגל , is 66. Six is the number of the cosmos. But why 12 stones, and why place them in a circle? The symbol is the same as that of Stonehenge and the New Jerusalem: it is a picture of the completed work of God. Just as there were 12 stones at Gilgal, representing the 12 tribes of Israel, so the New Jerusalem has 12 gates on which are inscribed the names of the 12 tribes of Israel.

The gematria for Gilgal, גלגל , is 66. The number which characterizes the cosmos is 6. World, γην, is 60, while the word cosmos, κοσμος, has the value of 600. The mile unit measures the cosmic intervals in terms of the number 6 as is demonstrated by the following:

137

Diameter of the sun .... 864,000 miles
$(6+6)$ x $(6+6)$ x 6000

Diameter of the moon .... 2160 miles
6 x 6 x 60

Diameter of the earth .... 7920 miles
$(6+6)$ x 660

Mean circumference of earth ..... 24,883 miles
12 x 12 x 12 x 12 x 1.2

Speed of earth around the sun .... 66,600 m.p.h.

It is interesting to note that the number 6 is both the sum and the product of all its factors, for $1+2+3=6$ and 1 x 2 x 3 $=6$. It is also worthy of note that the 144,000 who will be with the Lamb on Mount Zion are, as John saw in vision, *"redeemed from earth."* (Revelation 14:3) The earth is characterized by the number 6, and if we multiply 6 x 144,000 the product is 864,000, which is the number of miles in the diameter of the sun. Jesus said (Matthew 13:43) *"Then shall the righteous shine forth as the sun in the kingdom of their Father."* Those who are given this beautiful privilege, having received redemption and a heavenly reward for a life of faithfulness, are scripturally defined as *"saints."* The gematria for saints, αγιων, is 864. They not only figuratively *"shine forth as the sun,"* but they also bear the solar number. This heavenly condition of the saints was pictured by the Most Holy in the Tabernacle. The gematria for Most Holy, αγιων, is 864.

The Lamb who stands on Mount Zion will then be given another title, denoting his position of rulership and authority; he will be called Lord of lords, Κυριος κυριων, which bears the number 2280. The radius of the moon is 2280,000,000 feet and one side of a square of the same perimeter as the earth is 2280 MMi.

A square with an area of 86,400 units measures 294 on each side and 1176 around the perimeter. The number 294 is the value of εκκλησια, Church, while 1176 is the value of υιος μονολενης, only-begotten Son. In this way it is shown that the only-begotten Son, Jesus Christ, and the scripturally defined

138

Church, εκκλησια, are the same as the Lamb and his associates on Mount Zion.

In his description of the 144,000 on Mount Zion, the Apostle John called them *"virgins."* Revelation 14:4 *"These are they which were not defiled with women; for they are virgins. These are they which follow the Lamb whithersoever he goeth. These were redeemed from among men, being the first-fruits unto God and to the Lamb."* The language is, of course, symbolic. Virgins, παρθενοι, is 325; a number which bears a relationship to Stonehenge as well as to the Tabernacle.

325 = Virgins, παρθενοι
32.5 Roman paces—one side of a square of the same
  perimeter as mean Sarsen Circle
32.5 remens—radius of Bluestone Circle
32.5 Roman paces—diameter of Bluestone Circle
32.5 remens—diameter of Bluestone Horseshoe
.0325 miles—long side of Court of Tabernacle
.00325 miles—short side of Tabernacle (each side of
  Most Holy)

This little company of 144,000 are described as standing on Mount Zion. The gematria for Mount Zion, ορος Σιων, is 1500. It surely is not coincidence that each side of the New Jerusalem is 1500 miles, or that the diameter of the Bluestone Circle is .01500 miles, or that the distance from the Sarsen Center to the Heel Stone is 150.0 royal cubits. One side of a square drawn on the mean Sarsen Circle also bears this number, for it is .01500 miles. Surely the builder of Stonehenge had foreknowledge of the vision given to John on the Isle of Patmos.

The perimeter of the New Jerusalem is 6000 miles, each side being 7920,000 feet. A circle that contains the square would be roughly 6660 miles in circumference and a circle inscribed within the square would have an area of roughly 6,660,000 square MY. It is not coincidence that at Stonehenge the square of the distance from the Sarsen Center to the middle of the Heel Stone is 66,600 (258^2). The area of the Bluestone Circle is 666 MY and the average interval between the Sarsen uprights is .000666 miles.

The number of the cosmos, 6, is shown in nature by the phenomenon of the crystal, the snowflake and the cells of a honeycomb. Henry David Thoreau, exulting in the beauty of the snowflake wrote in his journal:

"The same law that shapes the earth-star shapes the snow-star. As surely as the petals of a flower are fixed, each of these countless snow-stars comes whirling to earth, pronouncing thus, with emphasis, the number six. Order, κοσμος . . . and they all sing, melting as they sing of the mysteries of the number six—six, six, six. He takes up the waters of the sea in his hand, leaving the salt; He disperses it in the mist through the skies; He recollects and sprinkles it like grain in six-rayed snowy stars over the earth, there to lie till He dissolves its bonds again."

Curiously enough, in geometry exactly six equal circles can be placed around the perimeter of an equal seventh, with the sides of each touching. And stranger yet is the fact that in the case of a sphere exactly twelve will cover a thirteenth so that each touches the center sphere and its four neighbors.

The number of the Beast

No discussion of the number 6 would be complete with the ignoring of the most well-known collection of sixes, *i.e.*, the number 666 of Revelation 13:18.

"Here is wisdom, let him that hath understanding count the number of the beast: for it is the number of a man; and his number is six hundred threescore and six."

In the original Greek text the number is spelled in letters, χξs or 600, 60, 6.* For centuries students of Scripture have puzzled over the meaning of the text. Many, including the author, have theories concerning the identity of Mister 666.

*At one time in the history of the Greek language the letter *vau* (s′) was in use. It carried the number value of 6. It later became extinct. Revelation 13:18 is the only passage of Scripture where *vau* is used.

Theories can be nice things to have around; they are comforting to the ego, but what facts do we have upon which to build theories?

It is indeed interesting to note the number values for the following Biblical phrases:

2 Thessalonians 2:3
"The man of sin, the son of perdition" = 6 x 666
ανθρωπος ανομιας υιος της απωλειας

2 Thessalonians 2:9
"according to the operation of Satan with all power
and signs and wonders" = 6 x 666
κατ ενεργειαν του Σατανα εν παση δυναμει και
σημειοις και τερασιν

"wonders" = 666
τερασιν

Luke 12:31
"the kingdoms of this world" = 2 x 666
βασιλειας οικουμενης

John 12:31
"Ruler of this world" = 7 x 666
αρχων του κοσμου τουτου

Since 6 is the number of the cosmos, the triple of sixes, 666, has reference to material as opposed to spiritual activity. Whereas 864 is a solar number, 666 pertains to the earth. A circle with a diameter of 7920 miles (diameter of the earth) has an area of 666,000 square MMi. The area of the Bluestone Circle is 666 square MY and the area within the wall of the New Jerusalem measures 6,660,000,000 square MY.

The phrase which the Apostle John used to give the number of the beast is translated *"and his number is six hundred threescore and six."* The original Greek text reads και ο

141

αριθμος αυτου χξς'. When we add the number values of all the Greek letters, the phrase becomes 2368, the identical number of Jesus Christ, 'Ιησους Χριστος. It does not seem to be coincidence that the phrase which John used becomes the number equivalent of Jesus Christ, for the beast is, in fact, the imposter of Jesus Christ. This is further demonstrated by the number value of the title, Image of the Beast, which is another name for the beast who is identified with the number 666. Image of the Beast, η εικων του θηριου, is 2260, but curiously enough, 2260 is also Son of Man, ο υιος ανθρωπου. The Man of Sin, ο ανθρωπος της ανομιας, also bears the number 2260. Again, a seeming relation between 666, the number of the beast, and 888, the number of Jesus is found in 2664, for 4 x 666 = 2664 while 3 x 888 = 2664. And 2664, as discussed in Chapter 7, was found to be the square of 51.6 which relates to the Tabernacle and the distance from the Sarsen Center to the Heel Stone. With the addition of one unit (2665) it becomes God the Father Almighty, Θεος ο πατηρ παντοκρατωρ.

2368 = Jesus Christ, 'Ιησους Χριστος
2368 = *"and his number is six hundred threescore and six,"*
  και ο αριθμος αυτου χξς'

2260 = Man of Sin, ο ανθρωπος της ανομιας
2260 = Son of Man, ο υιος ανθρωπου
2260 = Image of the Beast, η εικων του θηριου

2664 = 3 x 888
2664 = 4 x 666

The use of the same number by an imposter is again found in the use of the name Babylon in Revelation. Babylon, Βαβυλων, is 1285, while the true city of God, The Holy City Jerusalem, η αγια πολις 'Ιερουσαλημ, is also 1285.*

---

*The ancient city of Babylon was a square with a perimeter of 56 miles, which could correspond to the 56 Aubrey Holes of Stonehenge, while Nebuchadnezzar's palace, which included the famous Hanging Gardens, had a perimeter of 31,680 feet, corresponding to the circumference of the Sarsen Circle. Could this have been an attempt at counterfeit?

In Revelation 11:8 that great city which is called *"Sodom and Egypt,"* Σοδομα και Αιγυπτος, is 1480, while the number of Christ, Χριστος is also 1480—again demonstrating that the same number applies to the true and the false.

The number of the beast as given in the Greek text is χξς'. The abbreviation for Christ is Χς. The ancient symbol of the serpent was the Greek letter ξ. (It even looks snaky.) Therefore, the Greek letters which John used becomes Christ with the heart of a serpent. Thus it seems evident that Mister 666, whoever he may be, is an imposter, claiming the authority of Christ. He bears a number which is earthly, just as John said: *"It is the number of a man."*

Sun, Earth and Moon

Many years ago, when I was but a young teenager, it was explained to me that the geometry of the Great Pyramid revealed earth's distance from the sun. To me it was a fantastic bit of knowledge—a fact which opened up a lifetime of interest in the study of the Pyramid. As a natural result, when facts concerning the relationship of Stonehenge to the sun and moon became available, my curiosity was aroused. Could this ancient stone monument also hide such fantastic facts? If it did, where would we look? What is there at Stonehenge that points to the sun?

Every year, on the morning of summer solstice, crowds gather at Stonehenge to watch the sunrise. It has become the tradition of centuries. To one standing in the center of the Sarsen Circle, the rising sun on the morning of summer solstice appears to be perched atop the Heel Stone. The whole orientation of the monument is built around this alignment. The Heel Stone was once called the Sunstone, for this reason. The circles of the monument, on the other hand, seem to pertain to the earth. Could the separation of the Heel Stone from the rest of the monument be telling us something?

Out of simple curiosity, I multiplied the distance from the Sarsen Center to the base of the Heel Stone (256 feet) by the number of days in the solar tropical year, and to my complete delight, found that the product times 1,000 is the mean distance from earth to the sun. (256 x 365.242 = 93,500.00) The mean distance from earth to the sun is about 93 million miles. Obviously, the placing of the Heel Stone at that precise distance was not by accident; it was engineered by one who knew the geometry of the universe!

William Petrie, father of Professor Wm. Flinders Petrie, was the first to suggest that the height of the Great Pyramid should, in some way, indicate earth's distance from the sun. It seemed a logical suggestion, since the apex pointed upward toward the sky, and the most prominent thing in the sky is the sun. He based his suggestion on a discovery previously made, that the perimeter of the structure's square base at its socket-level agrees in measure with the number of days in the solar tropical year and also that the vertical height of the monument is equal to the radius of a circle whose circumference is the same as the perimeter of the square base. He felt that the Pyramid's topstone may very well represent the sun and the perimeter of the base represent the orbit of the earth around the sun. He concluded, therefore, that the distance of the base from the Pyramid's topstone would, by some geometric or mathematical proportion, indicate the distance of earth's orbit around the sun. The measure from the socket level to the apex is 485 feet and when it is converted into miles it becomes .091856 miles, and when multiplied by 1000-million it becomes 91,856,000 miles, or approximately the distance from earth to the sun at its perihelion.

Stonehenge is a monument which records not only the movements of the sun, but also of the moon. Could earth's distance from the moon be shown there too? If so, where would we look? What is there at Stonehenge that points to the moon?

Every time the winter moon rises over the Heel Stone it is eclipsed. Thus the Heel Stone also becomes an important pointer to the moon. But from what point do we measure? Hawkins found the Aubrey Circle of 56 holes to be an efficient computer by which eclipses of the moon could be predicted. When the winter moon eclipsed, the "computer" would indicate it by a marker at Aubrey Hole 56. Measuring from a point on the axis parallel to this hole to the Heel Stone gives a distance of 67 royal cubits. When 67 is multiplied by the number of days in the synodic lunar year, 354, the product is 2370, and the mean distance from earth to the moon is 237,000 miles. The builder of Stonehenge had an amazing knowledge of the universe, a knowledge which was not to be available to man until the advent of modern technology!

It has been demonstrated that the geometry of Stonehenge relates to the geometry of the New Jerusalem and the universe; similarly, the Great Pyramid bears a remarkable relationship to the earth and moon. In Figure 28 is shown a diagram of the earth and moon situated tangent to one another so that their combined radii give a distance of 5040 miles. If the center point of earth were taken as the base of a pyramid, and the center point of the moon as its apex, with the sides of the base touching the extremity of the circle, the angle of that pyramid would be 51°51', the same as the famous angle of the Great Pyramid. In other words, the Great Pyramid was constructed on the geometry of the earth and moon.

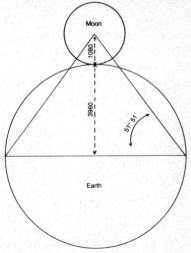

Figure 28

STONEHENGE...A CLOSER LOOK

Pythagoras and the Moon

Most high school students today are acquainted with some of the discoveries and theorems of Pythagoras, the Greek philosopher and mathematician. His school of learning was both mystical and practical. To his followers he was thought of as a kind of magician, because he taught them that nature is commanded by numbers. There is a harmony in nature, he taught, a unity in her variety, and all nature has a language: numbers are the language of nature.

Pythagoras found that the harmony of music was simply a mathematical principle. He found that chords which sound pleasing to the ear correspond to exact divisions of the string by whole numbers. This discovery led him to believe that not only the sounds of nature, but all her characteristic dimensions must be simple numbers that express harmonies. For example, he felt that we should be able to calculate the orbits of heavenly bodies by relating them to musical intervals. To him it was the music of the spheres. He felt that the world of sound and vision is governed by numbers.

But of all his discoveries and philosophies, whether fact or fancy, one enduring theorem has come down to us, and is used by every mathematician today. It is his concept of the right triangle. To Pythagoras, the basic example of the right angle in nature is the crossing of gravity with the horizon. He gave us the theorem that the square on the hypotenuse of a triangle is equal to the squares of the two sides if, and only if, the angle they contain is a right angle: $a^2 + b^2 = c^2$. The simplest form of the right triangle is the 3:4:5 triangle which is found to be in complete harmony with nature and the universe because $3 + 4 + 5 = 12$. To this day the theorem of Pythagoras is considered the single most important theorem in the whole of mathematics, because what he established is a fundamental characterization of time and space, and the laws that bind the universe. Pythagoras had found a truth, but the application of it was planted in the universe, from the beginning of creation.

As shown in Figure 28, when the circle of the moon is placed tangent to the circle of the earth, the proportions of the

Great Pyramid can be constructed on their combined radii. However, when a square is drawn on the circle, as shown in Figure 29, some astounding facts come to view. The right triangle formed by the position of the squares is a 3:4:5 triangle. The hypotenuse of that triangle is 3600 miles, which relates to the number of days in the prophetic Biblical *"time"* (360). Perhaps Pythagoras was right; numbers do indeed seem to be the language of the universe.

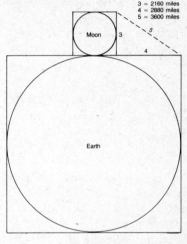

Figure 29

The number 360

That the hypotenuse of the most majestic of all 3:4:5 triangles should be 3600 miles seems not to be accident or coincidence. The number 360 is a number used by the Creator in the definition of time and space. The Bible uses the word *"time"* to denote a period of 360 years. Thus in Revelation 12:14 the mention of *"time, times and half a time"* becomes 1260 years: time (360) + times (360 + 360) + half a time (180) = 1260. Similarly, the phrase *"times of the Gentiles"* used in Luke 21:24 refers to a multiple of 360. To find how many

147

360s were meant we must go back to the book of Daniel and the story of Nebuchadnezzar (Daniel 4:25) and there we find the prophetic *"seven times."* Therefore the *"times of the Gentiles"* become a period of 2520 years: 7 x 360 = 2520.

When did Gentile kingdoms begin to assume world dominion? The year was in the autumn of 607 B.C., when Nebuchadnezzar, who was yet only vice-gerent of Babylon's King Nabopolassar, conquered Assyria. At that time he also took the Jewish nation of Judah into captivity and from that date they became a vassal to Babylon, the first universal Gentile empire. If we add 2520 years to 607 B.C. the year 1914 A.D. would denote the end of the prophetic *"times of the Gentiles"*: –607 + 2520 = 1915, however we must subtract one year because there was no zero year between B.C. and A.D., giving the year 1914. Twice the *"times of the Gentiles"* becomes 5040 years, and the combined radii of earth and moon is 5040 miles.

The diameters of earth, sun and moon are all multiples of 360:

Diameter of sun............ 864,000 miles (2400 x 360)
Diameter of earth .... 7,920 miles (22 x 360)
Diameter of moon............ 2,160 miles (9 x 360)

The system of dividing a circle into 360 degrees harmonizes with the ancient calendars which consisted of 360 days. The Hebrew Scriptures give a clue to the belief that a 360-day year was used, giving 12 months of 30 days each. One evidence of this can be found in Genesis 8:3, 4. Here it is stated that the waters of the flood prevailed 150 days, ending on the seventeenth day of the seventh month. Since it was stated that the waters began on the seventeenth day of the second month, the only way 150 days would end on the seventeenth day of the seventh month would be on the basis of 30-day months.

The Hebrews were not the only nation to use the 360-day year. It was also used by the Chinese, Babylonians, Hindus, Persians, Assyrians, Egyptians, Greeks, Romans, and even the Incas of Peru and the Mayas of Yucatan. The seeming universal use of the 360-day year lends weight to the concept, held by many, that the earth was once on a 360-day solar cycle. It has been suggested by many that perhaps some global catastrophe effected a change in earth's speed of rotation. I suspect that if such a premise were true, it would have been the flood catastrophe of Noah's day which would have effected this change. This is based on the concept that earth's volume was greater while the vapor canopy surrounded it than after that vapor was changed to rain and fell to earth. Others, however, attribute the change in the solar cycle to an event in the 8th century B.C. This reasoning is, in part, based on the realization that in the 7th century B.C. five *Gatha* days were added to calendars. The Mayan year added five days and every fourth year another day, and called them *"the days of nothing,"* during which the people did nothing.

The numbers by which we measure time are commensurate with the numbers of Stonehenge, the New Jerusalem and the cosmos.

12 hours in ½ day
1440 minutes in one day
3600 seconds in one hour
86400 seconds in one day
8640 hours in one 360-day year

Emerson once said "Nothing is rich but the inexhaustible wealth of nature. She shows us only surfaces, but she is a million fathoms deep."

Zophar, one of Job's so-called comforters, attempted to express our limited knowledge of the mysteries of the universe and of the Creator:

"But oh that God would speak, and open his lips . . . and that he would show thee the secrets of wisdom, that they are double to that which is." (Job 11:5, 6)

The one remaining stone of the great Central Trilithon dwarfs Bluestone No. 68. This giant sarsen is the largest hand worked stone in Britain, weighing 50 tons.

9

The Golden Section

The builder of Stonehenge had at his command an amazing knowledge of mathematics. This has been demonstrated by the development of the circles. It has been discovered that he also had access to the knowledge of the Golden Proportion. Since Renaissance times this proportion has been known as the Golden Section. In modern times this proportion has been designated by the Greek letter φ (pronounced phi). The ratio is 1:1.618. It can be obtained simply by dividing a line

A   B

at a point C

A   C   B

in such a way that the whole line AB is longer than AC in the same proportion as AC is longer than CB. Thus $\dfrac{AB}{AC} = \dfrac{AC}{CB} \doteq 1.618$

This equation, which appears to be simple, has profoundly affected art and architecture for thousands of years. Plato called it the most binding of all mathematical relations, and the key to the physics of the cosmos.

The Golden Section is best known in the figure of a rectangle. The Golden Rectangle is said to be one of the most visually satisfying of all geometric forms. The construction of the Golden Rectangle can be simply demonstrated thus:

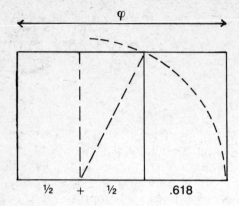

Figure 30

The properties of φ are interesting. It is a mathematical fact that $\varphi + 1 = \varphi^2$. It has also been demonstrated that the squaring of the circle, while insoluble by using the irrational number π, is closely resolvable as a function of the Golden Number φ. This is because $\dfrac{\pi}{2} \doteq \dfrac{2}{\sqrt{\varphi}}$, thus π can be usefully taken as $\dfrac{4}{\sqrt{\varphi}}$ (accurate to .01%).

The beautiful impression of harmony and perfect proportion which one sees in the Sarsen Circle is due to the incorporation of the Golden Number in its construction. The circle consists of 30 uprights; thus if we divide the circumference by 30 we obtain the width of one upright plus the interval. This turns out to be 10 feet 6½ inches. The height of the uprights plus their lintels is 16 feet 2 inches. Thus if we divide the height by one 30th of the circle, the resulting ratio is very close to 1.6, corresponding to φ.

152

This delightful proportion is found elsewhere in those lonely old stones. By dividing the height of the Great Central Trilithon by its width, the result is about 1.6. To obtain this proportion, the builders sacrificed some of the stability of the stones. Stone 56 of the Great Trilithon is buried to a depth of 7 feet 7 inches, while its partner, number 55, was sunk only to a depth of 3 feet. Because of the shallow foundation, stone 55 has fallen.

Another interesting demonstration of the use of φ at Stonehenge is in the relationship of the Sarsen and Bluestone Circles. The ratio between the squares of their radii is 1.6 to 1. This fact not only shows that the builder had access to φ but also to π, for they were able to calculate the area of a circle.

The use of φ at Stonehenge provides another corresponding link with the Great Pyramid, for the builders of that most remarkable of all ancient structures also had access to φ. It has been said that Herodotus was told by the temple priests that the area of each face of the Great Pyramid is equal to the square of its height. This interesting observation demonstrates that the Great Pyramid not only shows the π proportion, but also the φ proportion. The φ relation is found in the triangle formed by the height, half the base, and the apothem, which is the basic cross section of the structure.

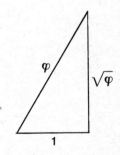

Figure 31

153

STONEHENGE...A CLOSER LOOK

Thus, once again, we find a basic link between these two ancient stone works. This similarity alone would not cause the observer to consider a common architect, for many structures, both ancient and modern, have obtained their harmony of design from the Golden Section. The Parthenon at Athens was built with this beautiful proportion. However, considering the antiquity of both Stonehenge and the Great Pyramid, and the numerous other correlations, many of which could not have been by chance, we have another evidence of a common architect. But who was he?

10

Who Was The Architect?

A 1977 television film, *In Search of Stonehenge,* suggested that whoever the builders of Stonehenge were, "they had help." The obvious implication being that the construction of that remarkable monument reveals an intelligence superior to that of man.

Theories and legends have come down through the ages but the mystery of those old stones still haunts the minds of all who have pondered their origin. A feeling of mystery is aroused at the very sight of Stonehenge. That monument, unique in all the world, seems to defy human reasoning; so the imagination takes over where reason fails.

One story that was invented in the fifteenth century attributes it to the work of the devil. It seems that the wizard Merlin wanted to build a stone monument on Salisbury Plain but the stones he wished to use were owned by an old woman in Ireland. Needing help, Merlin asked the devil for his assistance. The devil went to the old woman and offered to buy the stones. But the devil, of course, must be true to his stereotyped character. He tricked her. He offered her as much money as she could count during the time it took him to lift and prepare them for transport. Being gullible, as little old ladies are supposed to be, she eagerly accepted the bargain, thinking she would become rich. The devil handed her a purse filled with coins, but their values were rather difficult to count—four and a half pence, nine pence, thirteen and a half pence, etc. But as soon as she began to count, the devil told her to stop. The stones were bundled and ready to go. He picked them up, tossed them over his shoulder and flew off to Salisbury Plain.

Even the devil, I suppose, is not without his problems, for on the way the rope with which the stones were tied began hurting him, and he shifted the load to his other shoulder. Apparently even the devil makes mistakes, for while executing the grand shift in mid-air one of the stones worked loose from the bundle and fell into the Avon. (Tellers of the tale can even show us the stone which still lies partly submerged in the Avon.) It was midnight when he arrived at Salisbury Plain, a most appropriate hour. In the morning chill, just before dawn, the devil put the last stone into place. Standing back to admire his work, he said aloud, "No one will ever know how these stones came here, or from where."

Of such stuff are legends made! But legends have a strange effect upon people. Because of some unexplained and unexplored faculty of the human mind, it is easier and more desirable to believe fiction than fact. But surely no one today would believe such a fabricated tale, or so it might seem, until we find the voluminous material which is being written and published today about the role of the devil and his demons in the building of Stonehenge. The basic story is the same; it is only dressed up in its Sunday clothes and made to appear credible.

Many theories have come down through the centuries regarding the origin of Stonehenge. In the seventeenth century studies were made of the monument. George Villiers, Duke of Buckingham, was residing with King Charles I at Wilton, which is a few miles from Stonehenge. Probably while horseback riding on the Plain he saw the monument and spoke of it to the king. Stonehenge was at that time part of a farm owned by Mary Trotman. The king was anxious to see the curious stones, and wanting to ask questions of one who should have understanding of such things, he brought along his chief architect, Indigo Jones. As they looked at those lonely stones, the king asked him for an explanation of what they were and who erected them. Indigo Jones had to say something. One does not get to be the king's chief architect unless one has answers for such things. He replied, "It is a Roman work in the ancient Tuscan style, dedicated to the god Coelus."

Stonehenge, however, had made a deep impression upon the architect, and he took measurements from which he made drawings. He began to realize what all who have ever studied Stonehenge have eventually come to face—the architectural knowledge that its construction presupposed. He could not accept the legend of Merlin and the devil, nor did he believe that ancient Britons were knowledgeable enough to have built it. He therefore concluded that it was of Roman origin, and his drawings of the monument definitely reflect a Roman flavor.

In the year 1666 John Aubrey made a study of Stonehenge. His re-discovery of the 56 holes which surround the monument was an important advance in the knowledge of Stonehenge, and they have been named in his honor. However, Aubrey attributed the building of the monument to the Druids, even though he admitted that he was merely "groping in darkness." He recorded that in his day the stones were thought to have magical properties, and that the legend of Merlin and the devil was believed to account for its origin.

In the next century this suggestion of a Druid origin took shape and was published as fact. It was the work of William Stukely, a famous surgeon and close friend of Newton. The title of his book leaves no doubt of its author's conclusions that Stonehenge was built by the Druids—*Stonehenge, a Temple Restored to the British Druids*—and the book is full of that idea. He called the monument the cathedral of the "Archdruids."

Although Stukely's profession was medicine, he became completely enamored with Stonehenge and the Druids. He had a miniature Stonehenge built in his garden. He decided to become a minister and reconcile Christianity with the ancient religion of the Celts. Because of the enthusiasm and eccentricities of William Stukely, the concept that Stonehenge was a Druid temple has come down to us today and is believed by many as fact. What Stukely had failed to realize is that Stonehenge is immensely older than the Druids.

As early as 1793 James Douglas wrote that Stonehenge had been built long before the time of the Druids. In 1812 the tireless researcher, Sir Richard Colt Hoare, published a two-volume work, *The Ancient History of Wiltshire.* He attributed Stonehenge to the Britons and believed they used it as a meeting place for civil and religious assemblies.

William Cunningham assisted Hoare in his work of excavation at Stonehenge. They found under Station Stone 94 some cremated remains, which caused them to believe the Stations were grave mounds.

William Matthew Flinders Petrie took measurements of Stonehenge in 1877. On the basis of astronomical considerations, he dated the monument at the year 730, plus or minus two hundred years.

By the end of the nineteenth century much had been learned about Stonehenge; however, its origin still remained unknown, and theories abounded. The idea of Stonehenge being purposely oriented to the summer sunrise began to make its presence felt. In 1901 Sir Joseph Norman Lockyer, Astronomer Royal, attempted to date the monument by the use of the summer solstice sunrise azimuth. He proposed a construction date of 1680 B.C., plus or minus two hundred years. Later he changed his calculations and proposed 1840 B.C., with the same margin of error, for the construction date.

In 1950 R. J. C. Atkinson, professor of archaeology at the University College of South Wales at Monmouthshire, made an interesting discovery. While working with a team of archaeologists, making excavations at the site, he found a piece of charcoal in the bottom of Aubrey Hole 32. The discovery itself was nothing extraordinary, except for the fact that the radiocarbon dating method had just been developed and the little piece of charcoal provided an excellent sample to be tested by the new method. Atkinson found that his little piece of charcoal was dated at 1848 B.C., with a margin of error plus or minus 275 years. But what is radiocarbon dating and can it be relied upon for accuracy?

Radiocarbon dating

The concept and method of radiocarbon dating was made

possible by developments in atomic physics. Its basic principles are ingeniously simple.

When atomic physics was first being investigated in the early decades of this century, it was discovered that the earth is constantly being bombarded by small, sub-atomic particles. Since these particles have their origin outside the solar system, the bombardment is called *cosmic radiation*. These particles are so small that they are only detectable by methods of atomic physics. When they come into contact with earth's atmosphere, they set off a number of atomic reactions. One of the results of this is the production of small quantities of radiocarbon in our atmosphere, particularly at high altitude.

Radiocarbon (C-14) is a rare variety of the common element carbon (C-12), and it behaves chemically in just the same way as ordinary carbon. It is slightly heavier; the atoms weighing fourteen units instead of twelve.

Both carbon-14 and carbon-12 atoms combine chemically with oxygen, giving carbon dioxide. This is distributed throughout earth's atmosphere and is taken up by plants during the process of photosynthesis by which they form their structure. Animals eat the plants, forming a complicated food chain, resulting in the fact that the bodies of both animals and plants contain the same proportion of carbon-14 as does the atmosphere.

Carbon-14 differs from the common carbon-12 in that it is radioactive. It decays spontaneously at a slow rate, giving off a small sub-atomic particle called an electron. The process changes carbon-14 into a different element, nitrogen. This radioactive decay takes place in such a way that half of a given sample of radiocarbon has disappeared after a time of about 5,500 years.

The amount of carbon-14 created in the atmosphere by cosmic radiation was thought to be exactly balanced by its loss through radioactive decay so that the ratio of carbon-14 to carbon-12 in the atmosphere would remain a constant. This is picked up by living plants and animals, and so long as they live, they contain the same proportion of carbon-14 as the atmosphere. But when a plant or animal dies, it drops out of the food chain. It becomes a closed system. Its radiocarbon decays radioactively, but is no longer replenished—the balance is no longer maintained.

The process of radiocarbon dating depends on four assumptions:

1. That radioactive decay of carbon-14 takes place at a constant rate, regardless of physical or chemical conditions.
2. That the sample to be dated has not been contaminated since its death.
3. That the proportion of radiocarbon in all living things at a given time is a constant.
4. That the concentration of radiocarbon in earth's atmosphere has remained constant through time.

In recent years it has become known that the fourth assumption is not correct—the concentration of radiocarbon in earth's atmosphere has not been a constant. Before about 1000 B.C. the deviations are so great as to make radiocarbon dates significantly in error. Dates prior to the Flood catastrophe are unreliable because of the great changes which took place in earth's atmosphere. Thus radiocarbon dating has been found to be unreliable.

Realizing this, scientists have devised a method known as the tree-ring calibration of radiocarbon. Dendrochronology, the method of tree-ring dating, is based on the principle of counting the rings in a tree stump or core sample, and thereby determining the age of the tree. A sample thus dated is then radiocarbon dated, to see if the two dates agree. If the four assumptions of radiocarbon dating are correct, the two dates will be the same. It turns out that they are not.

By performing large numbers of radiocarbon tests upon core samples from the bristlecone pine, a graph has been constructed which now may be used to convert radiocarbon dates to the true tree-ring dates. This is called the tree-ring calibration of radiocarbon. This graph can be used with considerable accuracy.

From the available samples which have been radiocarbon dated, Atkinson came to the conclusion that Stonehenge was built in the seventeenth century B.C. in radiocarbon years. By using the calibration curve, this would give a construction date of between 2100 B.C. and 1900 B.C. in calendar years.

In search of the Architect

Atkinson suggested that surely the designer of such a marvelous structure deserves the title of architect. Then he added that it almost certainly would have been a man who was familiar with the Mediterranean world.*

Hawkins suggested that perhaps some "master designer" may have come from the Mediterranean area to Britain.† He reasoned, as did Atkinson, that some "one man" brought the necessary knowledge from elsewhere, since no predecessors, or trial building projects, have been found in Britain. Such advance concepts in complex structure, as well as the building techniques, could not have risen from nothing. Thus the evidence pointed to a Mediterranean origin.

R. S. Newall exclaimed that the more he studies Stonehenge, the more does he "admire the man, whoever he was" who conceived and carried out such a mighty work with such exactness."‡

Fernand Niel reasoned that because of the unique character of Stonehenge, it is obvious that it is the work of a "single man." He suggested that this man was foreign to Britain.* †He felt that perhaps the people of the Wessex Culture in ancient Britain erected the stones, but none of them conceived the plan. Reasoning as did Atkinson and Hawkins, he suggested that the architect came from the Mediterranean area, for only there could one have access to enough geometry, architecture and astronomy to design such a complex monument. Evi-

---

*R. J. C. Atkinson, Stonehenge and Avebury, Her Majesty's Stationery Office, London, 1959, p. 22.

†Gerald S. Hawkins, Stonehenge Decoded, Dell Publishing Co., Inc., New York, 1956, p. 51.

‡R. S. Newall, Stonehenge, Her Majesty's Stationery Office, London, 1959, p. 28.

* †Fernand Niel, The Mysteries of Stonehenge, Avon Books, New York, 1974, p. 198.

dence that the Wessex Culture had connection with Egypt has been unearthed in their burial grounds, where small blue beads have been found, and upon close examination were shown to have been made in Egypt. Niel also suggested the idea of a "master builder," one who had knowledge prodigious for his time. With the abundance of evidence at hand, who can doubt the existence of such a master?

Atkinson felt that Stonehenge is evidence that the concentration of political power, for a time, was in the hands of a single man. Surely he must have been a master. But what man, regardless of his education, knowledge or political power could have known the history of mankind in advance, and monumentalized it in stone in such a unique way as to synchronize it with the risings and settings of the sun and moon? What man, without the aid of modern technology, could have known the geometry of those spheres? What man could have known the speed of earth's orbit around the sun? What man, at that point in time, could have known the geometry of the New Jerusalem which was not given to John in vision until 90 A.D.? What man could have known the year in which a divine law would be given to Moses, or the very day that Jesus would die upon a cross, or that the nation of Israel would begin to be reborn? What man could have known the only latitude in the northern hemisphere where the risings and settings of the sun and moon would trace the pattern of a rectangle, or that the diagonal of that rectangle would point directly to the Great Pyramid? Search as we may, no man can be found who possessed such knowledge!

Who placed the earth, sun and moon in their respective positions? Who devised the dimensions of each? Who set the speed of their orbits? Who knew in advance the year of the giving of the law to Moses, and the day that Jesus would die on the cross, or the year of Israel's liberation? Who gave the vision of the New Jerusalem to John on the Isle of Patmos? The answer is obvious—the Creator! The Jews called him Jehovah. He alone could have known in advance the whole history of man. He alone could have been the Architect of a monument that would so intricately relate to his universe and his eternal plan.

As if it were not enough that the Creator should reveal the geometry of his universe and the time features of his eternal plan by those eloquent stone circles on Salisbury Plain, he also placed his name there. It contains his *signature,* if you please!

The most perfect arrangement of stones in the whole monument was the beautiful ring of lintels which topped the Sarsen Circle. Its beauty of perfection could only have been fully appreciated by one looking down upon them. A perfect circle represents eternity, for a circle has neither beginning nor end. *"From everlasting to everlasting thou art God,"* said the Psalmist. He had neither beginning nor will his existence ever come to an end. This beautiful ring of lintels bears a mean circumference of 260 remens. The gematria for Jehovah, יהוה , is 26.

When God spoke to Moses at the burning bush (Exodus 3:14) he identified himself as *"I am that I am."* I am, אהיה , is 21. But he repeated it, thus the repeated number becomes 2121. There are 2121 square royal cubits in the area of a square of the same perimeter as the mean of that perfect ring of lintels.

Should we think it strange that those stones which have endured the ravages of time and the vandalism of man would have a divine Architect? In view of all the evidence, we would think it strange if it did not.

The Creator had to have an earthly representative, a foreman, if you will, for carrying out the project. As Atkinson has suggested, he would have been a man of great political power and influence, and one who was respected as in control, for the physical necessities for the construction of such a monument are staggering to the imagination. Who was he?

In finding the identity of such a man, it is necessary that we reason from the known to the unknown. This method, known as inductive reasoning, does not always produce facts. Since evidence points to Jehovah as the Architect, do we find anyone in the Bible who fills the necessary requirements for the builder? In the necessary time frame we find one who does.

Shem, a son of Noah, lived from 2571 B.C. to 1971 B.C., which is well within the time framework for both Stonehenge and the Great Pyramid. Being a Patriarch, he would be looked up to and respected and, according to the modes of the time, would possess great political power. He fits the requirements which Atkinson describes. The date of his birth is shown by the alignment of the summer solstice high as viewed through the Moonrise Trilithon, thus hinting of his connection with Stonehenge.

All authors who have spoken of the builder have suggested that evidence points to one of Mediterranean origin. Shem also fulfills this requirement. Many students of the Great Pyramid suggest that Shem was the builder of that structure, which pre-dated Stonehenge by well over a hundred years. There is overwhelming evidence that the geometry of the one monument was known to the builder of the other.

Hawkins suggested that whoever the builder was, he had a "God of time." And surely the time features of God's eternal plan are marked in detail by those ancient stone circles.

11

Prophecy

"What is already past is not more fixed than the certainty that what is future will grow out of it."—G. B. Cheever

Well said! There is a difference, however, between observing that which grows out of the past, and predicting it. To be able to predict future events requires a certain amount of omniscience which the author does not possess. The suggestions presented in this chapter are merely the results of inductive or deductive reasoning, as the case may be. And with such reasoning the author, of course, goes out on a limb while every reader holds a saw.

It is a fixed law, as Cheever observed, that what is future will grow out of what is past. For this reason Stonehenge becomes the focal point of history, for on that lonely plain in southern England the past, present and future meet. Those timeless stones still tell the time, and the purpose for which they were intended must yet be fulfilled. Come, walk with me again amid those ancient stones, those silent sentinels, and listen to their voice. It is the voice of ages past, the language of today, and the songs of all our tomorrows.

The night is dark and there is a damp chill in the air as it hangs heavily over those silent stones. It is the night of winter full moon and as the first light trembles on the night, we are aware that something is different; something has happened to the moon. It rises slowly and rests, as it were, atop the Heel Stone. It is only half a moon! The shadow of earth is slowly falling over it—the moon is eclipsed!

If we were to stand in the center of Stonehenge every time the winter full moon rises over the Heel Stone, we would see the same strange sight. Every time the full moon of the winter solstice rises over the Heel Stone it is eclipsed.

The alignment of this winter moon is identical to the alignment of summer solstice sunrise. It is 0° from the axis on the Aubrey Circle. If the Aubrey Circle, as suggested, represents the 7,000-year cycle and the sunrise alignment marked the date of Autumn 4127 B.C., then it follows to a conclusion that the winter moon alignment completes the cycle and represents the Autumn of 2874 A.D. The last thousand years or seventh millennium of the cycle would begin in Autumn of 1874. It is earth's great thousand-year day of which the Apostle Peter spoke.

> *"One day is with the Lord as a thousand years, and a thousand years as one day. . . . But the day of the Lord will come as a thief in the night; in the which the heavens shall pass away with a great noise, and the elements shall melt with fervent heat, the earth also and the works that are therein shall be burned up. . . . Nevertheless we, according to his promise, look for a new heavens and a new earth, wherein dwelleth righteousness."* (II Peter 2:3-13)

Obviously the Apostle was using pictoral language, graphically illustrating the destruction of earth's evil order of things and the establishing of an order of righteousness.

The Bible abounds with prophecies concerning this thousand-year day. If this seventh millennium is so important in Scripture, what is there at Stonehenge which marks its beginning as being Autumn 1874? Surely the fulfillment of such an overwhelming evidence of prophecy would not be unmarked.

There are no stone alignments that point to this all-important date; neither are there any sun nor moon alignments. Would the divine Architect have left unmarked the date that heralds earth's great Millennium? Let's look again.

As has been noted, the angle of summer solstice to north, using the Sarsen Center, is the famous Pyramid angle—51°51'. But take a few steps from the Sarsen Center to the Aubrey Center. Now look north. The meridian through the Aubrey Center intersects the Aubrey Circle at precisely the date point of Autumn 1874 A.D. The beginning of earth's seventh millennium is not marked by a stone, nor by the moon, nor even by the mighty sun; it is indelibly fixed by the immovable line of the meridian. In the prophecies and pictoral language of the Bible, the direction or position of north represents the dwelling place of God. The line of the meridian through the Aubrey Center points toward God, marking the beginning of the age in man's history which was prophesied to be for the reconciling of man to his Creator.

The prophecies picture this day as having a turbulent and war-like beginning but ending in world-wide peace and prosperity, with man fully knowledgeable of his Creator and fully reconciled to him. Often in prophecy it is called the "third day" because it is the third thousand-year day from the event which made it legally possible, *i.e.,* the death of Jesus.

The vision which was given to John of the New Jerusalem is a prophecy of the full work of reconciliation of man to his Creator. It is, in fact, a model of the earth, its geometry being the same as that of earth but on a reduced scale. To traverse the full length of the New Jerusalem would be represented by a distance of 7,920,000 feet. On the third day following the death of Jesus, two of his disciples walked dejectedly to the little town of Emmaus. They were sad and discouraged. They had been with him for nearly three and one half years and many times had heard him speak of a kingdom of peace and righteousness on earth. They had great hopes for that kingdom. But now all their hopes and dreams had been hung cruelly upon a cross to die. As they walked along the dusty road to their little village they said, *"we trusted that it had been he which should have redeemed Israel: and beside all this, today is the third day since these things were done."* (Luke 24:21)

As they walked along a third person joined them and walked with them. They invited him in to have supper with them. He spoke words of comfort to their saddened hearts but they did not recognize him until he broke bread and then disappeared from their sight. In speechless astonishment they knew that it was Jesus! He was no longer dead! With hearts nearly bursting with joy and excitement they hurried all the way back to Jerusalem that night to tell the other disciples.

167

They found their friends in an upper room and as they breathlessly told all that had happened to them that evening, Jesus suddenly was there in the room with them. He comforted their anxious hearts by explaining the Old Testament prophecies to them which foretold of his death and resurrection and of his kingdom of righteousness which he would establish in the earth. *"Then opened he their understanding that they might understand the scriptures."* (Luke 24:45)

This story, with its pathos and joy, tells us something about the great prophetic third day—earth's seventh millennium. The two disciples walked to Emmaus: a distance of threescore (60) furlongs (Luke 24:13). Then they returned the same distance that same day. On that third day they walked a distance of 120 furlongs, which is 79,200 feet, and at the end of that day they received enlightenment of the scriptures. They walked, in symbol, the length of the New Jerusalem. The prophet Zechariah spoke of the enlightenment which would come at the end of that thousand-year day:

> *"And it shall come to pass in that day that the light shall not be clear, nor dark: but it shall be one day which shall be known to the Lord, not day, nor night: but it shall come to pass, that at evening it shall be light."* (Zechariah 14:6, 7)

Ezekiel's City

In the year 573 B.C. Ezekiel was given a vision concerning a temple and its environs. At the time he had resided in Babylon for a little over twenty-four years, having been taken captive when Nebuchadnezzar took King Jehoiachin from the throne of Judah and put him in prison at Babylon.

In vision, Ezekiel was transported to a high mountain in Israel and from this vantage point he saw a city below him to the south. He also saw a temple for which detailed measurements were given. Although much care was taken in the giving of the measurements, the temple was never actually built; it was only a vision. Many students of the Old Testament prophecies claim that this temple is prophetic of the time when the New Jerusalem vision will be fulfilled, thus suggesting a correspondence between these two visions given 662 years apart. If this is true we should expect to find a correspondence in the geometry of each.

The unit of measure for the city and temple was given in Ezekiel 40:5 and 43:13.

". . and in the man's hand a measuring reed of six cubits long by the cubit and a hand breadth . . ."
"The cubit is a cubit and a hand breadth . . ."

In Ezekiel 41:8 it was called the *"great cubit."* But what cubit was meant? The use of more than one cubit prevailed in Babylon at that time. Herodotus mentioned the use of the royal cubit and a shorter one called the moderate cubit. In the Mishna the moderate cubit is defined as six hand breadths or 144 barleycorns. This moderate cubit is generally accepted by historians and archaeologists as 18.14 inches, thus a hand breadth would be 3.02 inches. But the reed of six cubits with which the temple and city were measured is defined as using a cubit which was called a *"cubit and a hand breadth."* The moderate cubit of 18.14 inches with the addition of one more hand breadth would become 1.76 feet.* Six of these special cubits defined the length of the reed, or 10.56 feet. As has been observed, the number 10.56 is the number of feet in each lintel of the Stonehenge Sarsen Circle while 10,560,000 yards defines the perimeter of the New Jerusalem. This number, which is found to be the number by which Ezekiel's temple and city were measured, was also found to define the circumference of the Sarsen Circle, the diameter of its outer face and the circumference of the outer face of the Inner Bank.

10.56 feet = 1 reed of 6 great cubits
10.56 feet—length of each lintel
1056 feet—circumference of outer face of Inner Bank
105.6 feet—diameter of outer face of Sarsen Circle
105.6 yards—circumference of mean Sarsen Circle
105.6 yards—perimeter of a square drawn on Bluestone Circle
10,560,000 yards—perimeter of New Jerusalem

*See Appendix VI, The Great Cubit

STONEHENGE...A CLOSER LOOK

The cubit of a *"cubit and a hand breadth"*—1.76 feet—is also found to be a prominent Stonehenge number. The radius of the outer face of the Sarsen Circle is 17.6 yards and the diameter of the inner face of the Inner Bank is 176 royal cubits. The Bluestone Circle has an area of .176 square miles.

1.76 feet = 1 great cubit
17.6 yards—radius of outer face of Sarsen Circle
176 royal cubits—diameter of inner face of Inner Bank
.176 square miles—area of Bluestone Circle

The correlating of the measurements of the temple with Stonehenge and the New Jerusalem is fascinating for they are all commensurate with each other; but for reasons of space it will not be attempted here. I cannot, however, pass over without mention of the dimension of the Most Holy within the temple. In Ezekiel 41:4 it is defined as 20 cubits long by 20 cubits wide. Using the great cubit of 1.76 feet the Most Holy is found to be 35.2 feet each side. As already noted, 3.52 feet is the average interval between the uprights of the Sarsen Circle and is consequently 1/3 the length of each lintel. The diameter of the outer face of the Sarsen Circle is 35.2 yards and the circumference of the outer face of the Inner Bank is 352 yards. The title by which Jesus called himself, The Way, η $o\delta o\varsigma$, is 352. Thus the Most Holy of the temple in some way relates to Jesus.

This relationship is further shown by the perimeter of the Most Holy which is 140.8 feet. The gematria for Savior, $\sigma\omega\tau\eta\rho$, is 1408. The perimeter of a square drawn on the extreme circumference of the Sarsen Circle is 140.8 yards.

In Ezekiel 43 a description is given of the division of the land among the twelve tribes of Israel. This is still a part of the vision and relates to the time when the New Jerusalem prophecy will be fulfilled, *i.e.,* earth's great Millennial Day. A special portion of land was to be as an offering to the Lord. This measured 26,000 reeds long by 10,000 reeds wide. The side measured in feet would be 264,000 by 105,600. Thus the holy portion bears the number of The Truth, η $\alpha\lambda\eta\theta\eta\varsigma$, 264. The Psalmist David wrote prophetically of the time of earth's great Millennial Day and described it as a time when truth would accompany the qualities of mercy and righteousness.

"Mercy and truth are met together; righteousness and peace have kissed. Truth shall spring out of the earth; and righteousness shall look down from heaven." (Psalm 85: 10, 11)

David, again referring to this same prophetic day, exclaimed:

"He shall judge the world with righteousness and the people with his truth." (Psalm 96:13)

While in vision upon a high hill in Israel, as it were, Ezekiel saw below him a city, the dimensions of which are given in Chapter 48, verses 30 through 35. It is not surprising to find the measures of the prophetic city commensurate with the New Jerusalem, for they both illustrate the same thing. They illustrate earth's great Millennium. Thus the dimensions are also earth commensurate.

The city had twelve gates, three on each side, just as had also the New Jerusalem and on these gates were the names of the twelve tribes of Israel. Each side of the city measured 4,500 great cubits or 7,920 feet. Since the diameter of the earth is 7,920 miles it is obvious that the city becomes a model of the earth. The New Jerusalem was 7,920,000 feet in diameter.

Each side of the city was divided into three portions with a gate for each. These portions measured 2,640 feet, showing that it is surrounded by and encompassed with truth.

The perimeter of the city is 18,000 great cubits or 31,680 feet. Thus it is commensurate with the Sarsen Circle whose mean circumference is 316.8 feet and the New Jerusalem whose perimeter is 31,680,000 feet. This perimeter of 31,680 feet illustrates that the Lord Jesus Christ, Κυριος 'Ιησους Χριστος, 3168, will be its King, for he will be King of kings and Lord of lords. His number surrounds the city which will, in fact, belong to him by right of purchase. He purchased it with his life on Calvary's cross.

The city which Ezekiel saw in vision was given a name—

171

Jehovah-shammah, *"the Lord is there."* In view of all the wonderful correlation between this prophetic city and Stonehenge it seems hardly possible that the wonder could be multiplied by any significant denominator, yet, to my complete delight, the name Jehovah-shammah is found in that beautiful ring of lintels. The mean diameter of that perfect circle is 37.1 MY and the gematria for Jehovah-shammah, יהוה שמה, is 371.

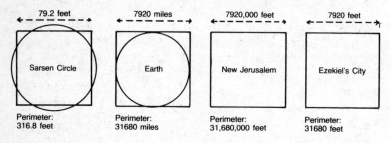

Figure 32

"Waters to swim in"

The temple given in vision to Ezekiel was never built. The present temple site in Jerusalem contains only the rubble and a retaining wall of their ancient sacred center. The beautiful Mosque of Omar which was built in 738 A.D. now occupies the temple grounds. To every Arab its is sacred; to every Jew it defiles the temple site.*

Why should one spot be so important? What is there about that one little piece of real estate that stirs the passions of both Arab and Jew and incites the worship of the Christian world?

The temple site at Jerusalem has become universally known as the place of union between God and man. It was on this

---

*The Mosque of Omar was built by Caliph Abd al-Malik in 738 A.D. to replace a temporary structure set up by Caliph Omar in 637 A.D.

hill that Abraham offered his son, Isaac, in sacrifice to God;
it was on this hill that King David built an altar and offered
sacrifice of thanksgiving to God; it was on this hill that Solomon built the beautiful temple. But why this hill?

Beneath this hill in Jerusalem, buried deep in the rock, lies
a vast underground spring. Should a way ever be opened,
pure water, the symbol of truth and life, would flow from
beneath the temple site!

Beneath the circles of Stonehenge also lies a powerful
underground spring. It is the convergence of several underground streams and fault lines. Guy Underwood, in his *The
Pattern of the Past,* shows a diagram of the remarkable pattern of underground water courses beneath the monument.

In the vision given to Ezekiel he saw waters flowing from
beneath the temple, bringing life once again to the Dead Sea.
He measured a thousand cubits and the waters were to the
ankles; he measured a thousand more cubits and the waters
were to the knees; he measured a thousand more and found
the waters were to this loins; *"afterward he measured a thousand, and it was a river that I could not pass over; for the waters
were risen, waters to swim in, a river that I could not pass over."*

The total distance measured was four thousand great cubits
or 7040 feet. The diameter of the inner face of the Inner Bank
of Stonehenge is 176 royal cubits; therefore the perimeter of
a square drawn on the circle would be four times this, or
704.0 royal cubits.

It has been demonstrated that the Sarsen Circle unmistakably relates to Jesus. When Jesus asked the Samaritan woman
for a drink of cool water from Jacob's well, he said *"whoso-
ever drinketh of the water that I shall give him shall never thirst;
but the water that I shall give him shall be in him a well of water
springing up into everlasting life."*

If the waters of the spring beneath Stonehenge should ever
surface, they would fill the area of the Inner Bank before
flowing northeastward toward the Avon. This inner bank is
made of the natural chalk which covers the plain. It could
well represent all mankind who will receive the waters of life
in earth's great Millennium. The waters that flowed from

Ezekiel's temple filled 7040 feet and if waters flowed from within the Sarsen Circle they would fill the 704.0 royal cubits of the square drawn on the Inner Bank.

The spring will probably never surface, yet the symbol which it provides will indeed be fulfilled in a reality.

Five more Bluestones

The discussion of the bluestones in Chapter 5 omitted the last one of the Bluestone Horseshoe, number 72A, and the remaining four of the Bluestone Circle, numbers 46, 47, 48 and 49. The alignments of these five remaining bluestones intersect the Aubrey Circle at dates which are future from this writing. It is for this reason that they are included in this discussion of prophecy.

In the Bluestone Horseshoe stone number 72A is not to be found. Archaeologists are agreed that it once stood in the place to which they have assigned it but it is, in fact, not there; thus it was never given a number. For purposes of identification we have labeled it 72A. Even without the evidence of its former existence in the horseshoe, it is reasonable to suppose that it once stood in the position indicated, for its counterpart on the other side of the horseshoe still stands today in its original position.

Assuming, then, that number 72A is authentic, let's draw a line from the Sarsen Center across the center of the stone and find its chronological position on the Aubrey Circle. Drawing the line as near to the center of the stone position as can be ascertained, the alignment is about 314.3° from summer solstice sunrise, giving a date of 1984 ± A.D. It is difficult to be exact since the stone does not exist.

Some may prefer to place the alignment at 1980 A.D. because of chronological parallels pointing to that date. Some suggest the date to which the alignment points is 1982 in which there will be an unusual conjunction of the planets. Others suggest it is pointing to the prophecy of Isaiah 23:11-17 which has been interpreted as predicting the establishment of a world church-state government in 1984. Any attempt of the author at an analogy would be preferential rather than factual. Since prophecy cannot be fully understood until it is finished, we will wait and see.

The last four stones are in the Bluestone Circle. Number 46 is a rhyolite stone standing in its original position. A line drawn from the Sarsen Center across this stone intersects the Aubrey Circle at the date point 2244 A.D. I take the liberty of eliminating the plus-or-minus from this date because this alignment touches the Aubrey Circle at the same exact point as another alignment which is not flexible.

As found in Chapter 3, the date 33 A.D. at Stonehenge corresponds to the date 33 A.D. in the Great Pyramid. The line connecting these two date points intersects the Aubrey Circle at exactly 2244 A.D.

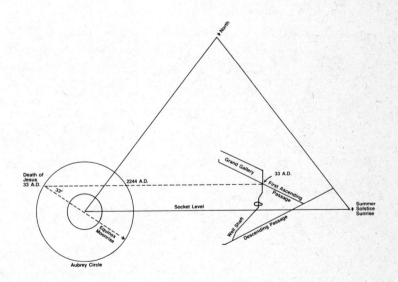

Figure 33

The date point 33 A.D. in the Pyramid marks the top of the Well shaft. As previously discussed, the Well was the only way of escape from the downward course of the descending passage, since the ascending passage was blocked by a huge plug made of solid granite. This way of escape represents mankind's only way of escape from the downward course that leads to death, *i.e.*, the ransom sacrifice of Jesus. The alignment with the Aubrey Circle from the bottom of the Well points to Enoch at 33½ years old—he illustrated Jesus. The alignment at the top points to Jesus at 33½ years old and more precisely to his death on April 3, 33 A.D. It follows that the remaining intersection of these alignments would point to the date of the application of this event, *i.e.*, life for mankind. This is what the ransom purchased.

Although it is a future date and although it is a safe rule that prophecy cannot be fully understood until it is fulfilled, I find the evidence most convincing that all mankind will have received the benefits of Jesus' sacrifice by the year 2244 A.D.

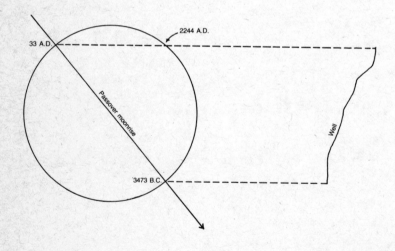

Figure 34

176

The convergence of these two alignments at Stonehenge pin-points the date; however, evidence in the book of Genesis confirms it. The ark saved Noah and his family from death during the flood catastrophe. The ark was the means of salvation to those it carried. It is, therefore, a fitting illustration of the means of salvation for all mankind, *i.e.,* the ransom. According to Genesis 7:10-13 the rain began on the seventh day. Earth's great seventh day, the seventh millennium, began in 1874. After 370 days Noah and all that were in the ark came out. They had been saved from destruction. Biblical time prophecies use the key: 1 day = 1 year. Using this key it is found that 370 years from 1874 A.D. gives the date 2244 A.D. After 370 days Noah and those with him received salvation from the great deluge. After 370 years mankind will have received salvation from Adamic death.

The next bluestone to be considered is number 47. The date of its alignment from the Sarsen Center is 2440± A.D. I do not know of any prophecies which point to this date. It is apparently pointing to something of importance during earth's great Millennium.

Bluestone 48 is severely inclined. It is of rhylite. The alignment of this stone from the Sarsen Center gives the date 2580± A.D. Again I do not know of any time prophecies relating to this date. I am however, convinced that both of these alignments point to dates which will be important to man.

The last bluestone in the circle is number 49. It is of dolerite and stands in its original position. The alignment from the Sarsen Center across the center of this stone gives an exact date, for it precisely traces the alignment of the winter moonrise high. The date to which it points is Autumn of 2730 A.D.

Earth's great Millennium spans a period of 1,000 years beginning in 1874 A.D. and ending in 2874 A.D. The date 2730 A.D. is exactly 144 years prior to the end of this great Millennial day. In view of the many uses of this number in the Bible, at Stonehenge and in the geometry of the universe, it is without hesitancy that I suggest the date 2730 A.D. will be an important year in man's experience, possibly concerning his ultimate reconciliation with his Creator.

The reconciliation of man to God is the purpose for which the great Millennial day was planned. By its close the prophetic New Jerusalem will have fulfilled its proposed function.

"And I John saw the holy city, New Jerusalem, coming down from God out of heaven, prepared as a bride adorned for her husband. And I heard a great voice out of heaven saying, Behold, the tabernacle of God is with men, and he will dwell with them, and they shall be his people, and God himself shall be with them, and be their God. And God shall wipe away all tears from their eyes; and there shall be no more death, neither sorrow, nor crying, neither shall there be any more pain: for the former things are passed away." (Revelation 21:2-4)

12

Concluding Thoughts

"He that answereth a matter before he heareth, it is folly unto him."—King Solomon (Proverbs 18:13)

The very existence of Stonehenge poses many questions— questions that have been asked by each new generation who beholds those lonely stones on Salisbury Plain. In the answering of those questions, the separation of fact from fancy sometimes becomes a little hazy. With a sincere desire to find answers I have attempted to collect all the data available about that marvelous old monument; much of which is the product of an attempt to explain the unknown in mystical language, or to consign its construction to a whim of the Devil. Many, however, have taken a more rational approach, looking at it through the eyes of archaeology, science, astronomy and engineering. Their approach was not an attempt to answer before finding the facts, therefore their discoveries are of great value in piecing together the *why,* the *how* and the *when.*

In the preceding chapters I have shown the remarkable correlation of Stonehenge with the Great Pyramid, the New Jerusalem, Ezekiel's City and the earth, sun and moon. Through all of these, one number has been outstanding. It is the beautiful number 3168, the gematria for Lord Jesus Christ. That wonderful, marvelous number is interwoven into all of God's creation. If any doubt remains regarding the role of the Creator in the design of all of these, it can be put to rest by the beautiful relationship of the number 3168 to the Pyramid passage angle—the Christ Angle.

179

STONEHENGE...A CLOSER LOOK

Pyramid passage angle—the Christ Angle

The passageways in the Great Pyramid are either horizontal or angular. All the angular passages slope at 26°18′. This has been called the Christ Angle because, as shown in Chapter 3, it is the basis for a right triangle whose dimensions define the dates of the birth, baptism and death of Jesus. At Stonehenge this angle is formed by the crossing of the Passover moonrise alignment with the azimuth from Stonehenge to Jerusalem (see Chapter 2), again showing its relation to Jesus, who died on the day of Passover moonrise. If any doubts linger regarding the authority for naming this the Christ Angle we have only to observe the remarkable relationship of this angle to the gematria of his name.

The number 3168 (Lord Jesus Christ, Κυριος 'Ιησους Χριστος) is the most prominent number at Stonehenge. The Creator has planted this number in the cosmos and used it to define the New Jerusalem and Ezekiel's City. One astounding fact remains—this remarkable number is used to define the Christ Angle!

The repetition of this number can best be shown by the list below:

3168 = Lord Jesus Christ, Κυριος 'Ιησους Χριστος
316.8 feet—mean circumference of Sarsen Circle
316.8 feet—perimeter of a square drawn on Bluestone Circle
316.8 yards—circumference of inner face of Inner Bank
3168 inches—one side of a square of same perimeter as outer face of Inner Bank
3168 inches—long side of Station Stone rectangle
31680 feet = 6 miles
31.68 feet = 18 great cubits
31.68 feet = 3 reeds
316,800 MMi—diameter of sun
31,680 furlongs—radius of earth
31,680 miles—perimeter of a square drawn on circumference of earth

3168 MMi—perimeter of a square drawn on circumference
   of moon
31,680,000 feet—perimeter of the New Jerusalem
31,680 feet—perimeter of Ezekiel's City

The Christ Angle is shown in the Great Pyramid as a right triangle. If we define the hypotenuse of a right triangle as 316.8 units and the base as 284 units, the angle thus formed is 26°18′—the angle of all the inclined passages in the Great Pyramid. The gematria for God, Θεος, is 284. The point where Lord Jesus Christ, Κυριος Ἰησους Χριστος, 3168 and God, Θεος, 284 converge is 26°18′.

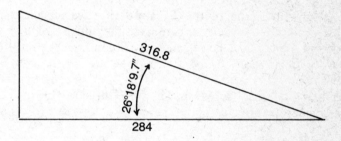

Figure 35

If this angle were carried out to a decimal the astounding fact is that it is less than four-tenths of a second from the precise passage angle, or a percent difference of .0005% (5/10,000%). Such accuracy overwhelms the comprehension; it staggers the imagination; it overflows like an avalanche upon the awareness that only the Creator himself could have designed it!

Pythagoras once observed that "numbers are the language of the universe." He had discovered a great truth. Numbers are, indeed, the language of the Creator!

181

STONEHENGE...A CLOSER LOOK

The Pyramid Angle

The Great Pyramid was once covered with beautiful white casing stones. Most of those original stones have been removed and used in the construction of buildings elsewhere. A few of those polished white stones at the base of the Pyramid were covered with sand and rubble and were thus not removed by vandals. When excavations uncovered them, much excitement was generated among Pyramidologists, for they revealed the true angle of its outer surface. This angle was found to be 51°51′. As already noted (Chapter 8) this angle was planted in the universe by the Creator. If the combined radii of the earth and moon were taken as the height of a pyramid, and the diameter of the earth as its base, the angle of that pyramid would be 51°51′.

The only stone in the Pyramid that was itself a perfect pyramid of the same proportions as the entire structure would be the topstone. It has been shown (Chapter 8) that this topstone represented Jesus. This was shown by the gematria of his name in relation to the base perimeter. (Base perimeter of topstone—2288.8 Pyramid inches. Christ the Lord, Χριστος η Κυριος, 2288.) This beautiful, perfect topstone also had an angle of 51°51′.

In the Bible, Jesus is called the Bridegroom, νυμφιος, 1270 (John 3:29); he is also called the Bread of God, ο αρτος του Θεου, 1995 (John 6:33) and the Lamb of God, αμνος του Θεου, 1615 (John 1:29). It is not by coincidence that these three numbers are the dimensions of a pyramid whose angle is 51°51′ for they show how that perfect pyramidal topstone is indeed a symbol of Jesus.

Again I can only stand in awe of the accuracy of this angle. The exact angle of the topstone, carried out to a decimal, is 51°51′14.3″. In the diagram above, the angle formed by the height and the base is 51°51′9.85298″ and the angle formed by the hypotenuse and the base is 51°51′19.75276″; thus the mean of the two becomes 51°51′14.8″ which is only five-tenths of a second from the Pyramid angle, or a percent difference of .0003% (3/10,000%). Coincidence has no place

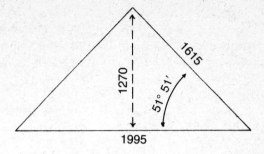

Figure 36

here: it was planned precision! I find no words with which to express the wonder and awe that floods over me. I can only quote the expression of this feeling by the great Apostle Paul:

"O the depth of the riches both of the wisdom and knowledge of God; how unsearchable are his judgments, and his ways past finding out!" (Romans 11:33)

Destruction and Restoration of Stonehenge

Stonehenge, that magnificent achievement of ancient man, that monument whose place rightfully should be beside the seven wonders of the ancient world, has suffered the ravages of time and the vandalism of man. How sad to realize that the marvelous perfection of its design lies prone and broken on the lonely Salisbury Plain. How did it acquire its present condition? Was its destruction deliberate, or was it solely due to the natural laws of entropy?

Let us first consider the probability of its ruin having been effected by natural causes. The awesome antiquity of those stones, alone, suggests deterioration by wind, storm, snow, heat and cold. Salisbury Plain is subject to high winds, especially in the winter. Consider the pressure of the wind alone! The average area of the face of an upright in the Sarsen Circle is about 90 square feet. A wind blowing at 45 miles per hour

183

STONEHENGE...A CLOSER LOOK

will exert a pressure of about 1,000 pounds against such a face, and in a severe windstorm the pressure could go above 3,000 pounds. Some of the stones were set into the ground at shallow depths, probably because stones large enough could not be found; and it was the above-ground heights that were essential to the precision of its geometry. Through centuries of precipitation, the ground level would gradually recede, leaving the foundations even more vulnerable to the pressures of wind and storm.

That natural forces have been the cause of some of the destruction of Stonehenge is evident from the fact that in the years since the monument began to be studied scientifically, and records have been kept, several stones have fallen from natural causes. Some have come to lean heavily and had to be made safe by pouring concrete into their foundations. It was recorded that on December 31, 1900, upright 22 of the Sarsen Circle fell in a violent storm, taking a lintel down with it. Since superstition has always been associated with those mysterious old stones, some took it as a portend of Queen Victoria's death, which occurred three weeks later.

Natural causes, however, have been only part of the answer to its present deplorable condition.

In the autumn of 1796 a band of Gypsies camped at Stonehenge. They dug a hole at the foot of the Moonset Trilithon (57-58) in which to place the foundation of their shelter. As winter spread across the Plain the Gypsies left. The constant filling of the hole with rain and snow weakened the foundations of the huge trilithon, and on January 1, 1797 it began tilting. During the next two days it gradually tilted more and more until on January 3 it fell toward the west. Fortunately there were no stones beneath its fall to break it, and the three stones of the trilithon remained intact. They were restored to their upright position in 1958.

Some of the stones, however, have been removed deliberately, for they simply are not there. Of the 30 original lintels in the Sarsen Circle only 6 are still in place, two are on the ground and 22 are missing. Stones of that enormity could not completely wear away from wind and rain; they were removed

184

by man, and sometimes with great effort. Let us consider, for example, lintel 105 which once topped uprights 5 and 6 of the Sarsen Circle. It is not to be found at Stonehenge. Its neighbors, 104 and 106, are still in place. There is no way that wind could have removed the lintel. The lintels were firmly secured with a mortise and tenon system atop the uprights, plus being secured at their ends by tongue-and-groove fittings. The deliberate removal of the lintel was difficult, laborious and dangerous. In order to remove this 7-ton boulder from its locked-in position, scaffolding would have to be erected on each side of the uprights so that the lintel could be raised. The only way of removing it would be to disengage it from its tongue-and-groove fittings by lifting it. It is evident that the removing of this lintel was, in itself, an engineering feat, involving the laborious and dangerous effort of many workmen. Had it been merely wanton destruction by vandals, uprights 4-5 and 6-7 would not be intact with their lintels.

In the British Museum is a manuscript entitled *Summary of Events in England, According to the Best Chronicles.* It contains a drawing of Stonehenge made by an anonymous draftsman in 1574. This valuable drawing shows uprights 13 and 14 of the Sarsen Circle still in place and joined by their lintel. Stone 13 is nowhere to be found today. Thus again we have evidence that some of the stones have been taken away from the site.

Two primary reasons have been proposed by historians for the removal of the stones. First, the many legends and superstitions about Stonehenge led men to believe that the stones had magical curative powers. Thus such stones would become prized possessions and coveted by powerful men. Second, the destruction of the monument and the removal of its stones is suggested by some to have been a deliberate act ordered by the church during the Roman occupation and the Middle Ages. If Stonehenge had become, by that time, a place of religious worship, it is understandable why the church would seek to destroy it.

Another line of reasoning lends itself to this discussion. If the Creator was, in fact, the Architect of Stonehenge, and if its design and construction were for the purpose of foretelling the future and recording history, would not the great adversary of God seek to destroy it?

Other Stone Circles

Stonehenge is unique among all the stone circles of Britain. Throughout England, Wales, Scotland and Ireland hundreds of monuments, burial mounds and stone circles can be found. Some are elaborate and some extremely simple, but none can be compared to Stonehenge. Whatever their function, and whatever their purpose, Stonehenge remains unique.

In 1976 an expedition sponsored by the Academy of Applied Science and The New York Times set out in search of the Loch Ness Monster, dubbed "Nessie." Elaborate underwater photographic equipment was set up in the murky waters of the loch, along with sonar systems, deployed to detect moving objects and to survey the bottom for carcasses or skeletons.

Off Lochend, at the northern end of Loch Ness, the sonar picked up a number of traces of circular patterns. Divers were sent into the dark waters to investigate. They reported finding stone circles from 15 to as much as 150 feet in diameter.

Obviously these circular stone arrangements were built at a time when this portion of the loch was dry land. In the millennia since, the level of the water has risen. (Presently it is about 50 feet above sea level.)

In north Wiltshire, lying among the elm trees of the Kennet valley, is another, yet less famous, circular arrangement of stones and chalk rubble. It is called Avebury. Today a small community has been built in its center and along its apparent axis. Little remains of it except the earthwork and ditch and a few stones—some of which were restored in 1939.

Stonehenge, existing in the environs of many similar structures, yet transcending them in every way is, again, like the Great Pyramid, whose singular magnificence exceeds the many other pyramidal shaped structures of Egypt. In Britain, as in Egypt, the others were used as places of burial.

In the five parishes around Stonehenge there are some 345 barrows or burial mounds. They are clustered around Stonehenge like the grouping of graves around a church. Some are circular mounds surrounded by a ditch, and some are more rectangular. They have been named *long barrows, bowl barrows, bell barrows* and *disc barrows,* denoting the shape and type of construction. Of all the barrows and burial mounds, one is unique.

Silbury Hill

One of the supposed burial mounds near Stonehenge is Silbury Hill. When it became apparent that the distance from Stonehenge to Silbury Hill is exactly 6 megalithic miles or 86,400 feet my natural curiosity about such things was aroused. So I attempted a study of that mammoth man-made mound. Why would it be connected to Stonehenge by such a significant figure as 6 x 14,400 = 86,400?

Silbury Hill is the largest man-made mound in Europe. Hawkins suggested that perhaps it might well be called the "great pyramid of Europe." This huge conical mound is not, however, pyramid-shaped, but circular, with a diameter at its base of about 600 feet and its flattened summit rising to a height of about 130 feet. It is surrounded by a ditch from which chalk was removed and used to construct the mound.

Excavations in 1968-69 revealed the marvelous engineering employed in its design and construction. It began with a central heap of gravel mixed with clay which was then capped by a turf stack within a ring of stakes. This in turn was covered with materials obtained from the flood plain of a neighboring stream. This was covered by a large mound of chalk dug from a surrounding ditch. Then a new ditch was begun farther out, and the chalk from it was piled on the mound, completely covering the first ditch as the diameter of the mound increased in width. This outer ditch remains today, usually filling with water in the winter.

The construction of Silbury Hill reveals an almost obsessive concern for stability by its builders. The construction materials have been laid in horizontal layers, each of which were divided into sectors by radial and circumferential walls of chalk blocks. It was so effectively protected against weather and erosion that the shape of the mound remains today nearly as it was built.

Legend suggests that it was the burial mound of some superlatively powerful Stone Age King. Indeed, some even go further and suggest that it may be the burial place of the builder of the greatest of British pre-historic monuments—Stonehenge.

No cremated remains have ever been found there. In 1777 attempts were made to explore the interior and a shaft was dug from the top to the bottom, but nothing was found. Still believing that the remains of some important personage would be found there, a tunnel was dug in 1849 from the south side to the vertical shaft, but nothing was found to give evidence of human burial.

Hawkins' suggestion that it was the "great pyramid of Europe" may have been more than a fanciful epithet for that ponderous pile of earth and chalk. It has been suggested by archaeologists that Silbury Hill dates back to the same era as Stonehenge, which is not much more than a hundred years after the Great Pyramid was built. If the suggestion in Chapter 10 that Shem could have been the builder of both of these magnificent monuments has merit, then there may be some credibility to the suggestion that the builder of Stonehenge is buried there. An enormous tomb, reminiscent of the Great Pyramid, would be fitting for such an important personage.*

Shem lived from 2571 B.C. to 1971 B.C. If, as has been deduced from the stone alignments as well as from the tree-ring calibration of radiocarbon dating, Stonehenge was completed in 1973 B.C., it would be reasonable to suppose that Shem (if he had been the builder) would have died there.

But Stonehenge lives on! Through the slow and steady passing of the centuries, it keeps its silent vigil on the lonely

---

*The prophet Zechariah, who spoke often of the Great Pyramid and related its top-stone to the Messiah, was honored by a pyramid having been placed atop his grave stone.

plain. Generations come and go, but those mute megaliths endure. There is none else to compare. It is all alone!

Stonehenge, by its solar and lunar alignments, by its geometry, by its relationship to the cosmos and to history, reveals its purpose and its Architect. It was not only an astronomical observatory but also a prophetic time device, whose Architect was the Creator.

After 4,000 years, the timeless monoliths of Stonehenge still stand bold against the summer sky.

photo by Thomas Gilbert

Appendix 1

Chronology

The chronology of man has long been in question. The era known as pre-history provides very little chronological data from which to draw analogies. There is one source, however, upon which we can rely. The Hebrew Scriptures give a careful and accurate record of the chronology of man which spans the time from his creation to the time when other histories begin to synchronize with it.

In the annals of the ancient kings many solar and lunar eclipses are recorded as having occurred. These are recorded in terms of the number of years of the reign of the king, *e.g., "In my fifth year, in the month Nisan,"* etc. The original cuneiform inscriptions of the kings of Assyria, Babylon and Persia are now housed in the British Museum, the Chicago Oriental Institute, and other museums, and have been translated into the major languages of today. In these inscriptions are found numerous records of solar and lunar eclipses, along with the current events of their day. These provide fixed dates upon which our chronology rests.

How do we arrive at fixed dates from eclipses? Fortunately the method is quite simple. The precision with which the Creator has placed the moon and the earth in their orbits makes it possible to determine the time of every solar and lunar eclipse throughout the past or future with accuracy to minutes and seconds. The computation of this is now done by computers, and books containing the computer print-outs can be obtained from any library.

The following is a brief outline of the chronology of man taken from the Hebrew Scriptures, from the annals of the kings of Assyria, Babylon and Persia, and from an eclipse calendar. In the interests of brevity only major links are shown, supported by a few of the eclipses which fix their dates. The details and voluminous proofs would fill a book.

Event	Years	Date B.C.
Creation of Adam	Autumn,	4129
"Adam lived 130 years and begat Seth" (Genesis 5:3)	130	3999
"Seth lived 105 years and begat Enos" (Genesis 5:6)	105	3894
"Enos lived 90 years and begat Cainan" (Genesis 5:9)	90	3804
"Cainan lived 70 years and begat Mahalaleel" (Genesis 5:12)	70	3734
"Mahalaleel lived 65 years and begat Jared" (Genesis 5:15)	65	3669
"Jared lived 162 years and begat Enoch" (Genesis 5:18)	162	3507
"Enoch lived 65 years and begat Methuselah" (Genesis 5:21)	65	3442
"Methuselah lived 187 years and begat Lamech" (Genesis 5:25)	187	3255
"Lamech lived 182 years and begat a son and called his name Noah" (Genesis 5:28)	182	3073
"Noah was 600 years old when the flood of waters was upon the earth." (Genesis 6:7)	600	2473
Total years of ante-diluvian man..............	1,656	
"Shem begat Arphaxad two years after the flood" (Genesis 11:10)	2	2471
"Arphaxad lived 35 years and begat Salah" (Genesis 11:12)	35	2436

"Salah lived 30 years and begat Eber" (Genesis 11:14)	30	2406
"Eber lived 34 years and begat Peleg" (Genesis 11:16)	34	2372
"Peleg lived 30 years and begat Reu" (Genesis 11:18)	30	2342
"Reu lived 32 years and begat Serug" (Genesis 11:20)	32	2310
"Serug lived 30 years and begat Nahor" (Genesis 11:22)	30	2280
"Nahor lived 29 years and begat Terah" (Genesis 11:24)	29	2251
"The days of Terah were 205 years and he died" (Genesis 11:32)	205	2046
Total years from the Flood to the death of Terah 427		

When Terah died God made a covenant with Abraham. (Genesis 12:1-7, Acts 7:2-4) From the covenant with Abraham to the Exodus was 430 years (Exodus 12:49-43, Galatians 3:17)	430	1615
Israel's wandering in the wilderness. (Deuteronomy 8:2)	40	
Israelites crossed the Jordan and into Canaan. (Joshua 4:19)		1575
From the entrance into Canaan to the division of the land. (Joshua 14:5-7, 10)	6	1569
The period when Israel was ruled by Judges. (Acts 13:20)	450	
The anointing of Israel's first king, Saul. (I Samuel 10:1 and 24)		1119
Division of Israel's monarchy into the nations of Judah and Israel. (I Kings 12)		999

Shalmanesser and Sargon of Assyria conquered Israel. (II Kings 18:11) (Assyrian Eponym Canon and annals of Sargon)	722
Recorded lunar eclipse in the 5th year of Nabopolassar of Babylon—occurred on April 22, 621 B.C. (Babylonian Chronicle)	621
Pharoah Necho of Egypt killed Judah's king Josiah. (II Kings 23:29-30) (Babylonian Chronicle)	609
Nebuchadnezzar of Babylon conquered Assyria and took Judah as a vassal nation, thus from that point in time Babylon became the first universal empire. This was in the 3rd year of Judah's king Jehoiakim. Nebuchadnezzar was vice-gerent of his father, Nabopolassar. This occurred in Nabopolassar's 18th year. (Daniel 1:1 and 2:37-38) (Babylonian Chronicle)	607
Nebuchadnezzar became king of Babylon upon the death of Nabopolassar, 1st Elul (September 7) 605 B.C. (Babylonian Cuneiform Inscriptions)	605
Judah's last king, Zedekiah, taken to Babylon by Nebuchadnezzar and killed. The Temple at Jerusalem burned. (II Kings 25:8)	586
Death of Nebuchadnezzar, October 7, 562 B.C. (Babylonian Chronicle)	562
Nebuchadnezzar succeeded by Evil-Merodoch (Babylonian Cuneiform Inscriptions)	562-560
Evil-Merodoch succeeded by Nergal-shar-usur August 13, 560 B.C.	560-556
On May 22, 556 B.C. Labashi-Marduk became king of Babylon. He reigned two months and the kingdom was given to Nabu-naid.	556

Nabu-naid's eldest son, Belshassar,
made co-regent   549

Cyrus' army entered Babylon on October 13,
539 B.C., killing Belshazzar and taking
Nabu-naid prisoner. Cyrus entered Babylon on
October 29, 539 B.C. From this date Medo-
Persia became the second universal empire.   539

Cyrus' decree for Jews to return to Jerusalem
and rebuild the Temple. (Ezra 1:1) From the
beginning of Babylonian captivity until the
decree of Cyrus was 70 years. (II Chronicles
36:21 and Jeremiah 29:10)   537

Death of Cyrus and accession of Cambyses.   530

Cambyses takes his own life—accession of
Darius I.   522

Restoration of the Temple at Jerusalem in the
6th year of Darius I. (Ezra 6:15) From the
burning of Solomon's Temple to the rebuilding
was 70 years. (Zechariah 1:12 and 7:1-5)   515

Reign of Darius I is astronomically fixed by
the recorded lunar eclipse in his 20th year
(November 19, 502 B.C.)   502

Recorded lunar eclipse in 31st year of Darius I
(April 25, 491 B.C.)   491

Death of Darius I and accession of Xerxes
(Ahasuerus)   486

Reign of Xerxes (Ahasuerus) is astronomically
fixed by a recorded solar eclipse in his 6th year
(October 2, 480 B.C.) which occurred nine days
after Xerxes' defeat in the battle of Salamis.   480

Esther became queen 10th month of 7th year of Xerxes (Ahasuerus).	478
Esther delivers the Jews from massacre in 12th month of 12th year of Xerxes (Ahasuerus). (Esther 9:17)	473
In Xerxes' 19th year Cimon of Greece made war with Persia. Xerxes' forces were severely beaten.	466

For those who assign only 11 years to the reign of Xerxes it should be noted that a cuneiform tablet found at Persepolis is dated the 20th year of Xerxes. This document is numbered A23253 at the Oriental Institute of Chicago.

Xerxes assassinated in his bedchamber by Artabanus	465
Artabanus (a usurper to the throne of Persia) attempted to rule by making the young teenager, Artaxerxes (son of Esther) his puppet king. After 7 months he attempted to kill Artaxerxes, but in the conflict, Artabanus was killed. Therefore the accession year of Artaxerxes was 464 B.C. and his first year began 463 B.C.	463
Nehemiah's commission to rebuild the walls of Jerusalem, 1st month (Nisan), 20th year of Artaxerxes. (Nehemiah 2:1-8)	444

The prophecy of Daniel 9:25 spans the time from the commission to rebuild the walls of Jerusalem to the death of Messiah. This prophetic period of *"69 weeks,"* (as with all time prophecies), must be computed on the basis of *prophetic* time (360 days per year. 1 day = 1 year). Breaking this down into units of one day; one prophetic day is equal to .9856478 of a solar day (360 ÷ 365.242 = .9856478). Thus one prophetic week becomes 6.8995 days (7 x .9856478 = 6.8995). The 69 weeks of Daniel's prophecy becomes 476 solar years (69 x 6.8995 = 476). The precision with which this prophecy foretells the death of Jesus is accurate to the month. Nehemiah was given the commission to rebuild the wall of Jerusalem in Nisan of 444 B.C., and 476 years from that date brings us to Nisan of 33 A.D. Jesus died on 14th Nisan, 33 A.D.

476 solar years = 69 prophetic weeks
Nisan <u>444</u> B.C., commission to rebuild wall
        32
   +   1 (add one year because there is no zero year
              between B.C. and A.D.)
Nisan   33 A.D., death of Jesus

The diagram below shows the transition from B.C. dates to A.D. dates, and it is easily seen that the zero year is missing.

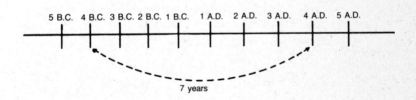

Figure 37

197

Appendix II

The
Centers

Nothing has yet been found at Stonehenge to mark the exact cetner of the Sarsen Circle, not even a post hole. Perhaps its center, during construction, was never marked on the ground. It would almost seem as if the builder wanted the true mathematical center to be lost. Skilled observers, such as Wm. Flinders Petrie, found three or four possible centers.

One method of finding the center is by crossing the diagonals of the Station Stones. The point of intersection would mark the center, as shown in the diagram below. Using this center, a circle can be inscribed which would touch the inner faces of the uprights of the Sarsen Circle. Since this point also rests on the observation line of the summer solstice sunrise, the axis of symmetry, it seems to have been the center intended by the builder.

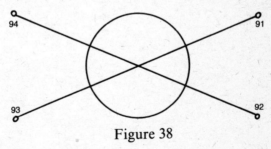

Figure 38

Finding the center of the Aubrey Circle is more difficult, for the diagonals from the four Stations do not intersect it. Attempts to locate it by the positions of the Aubrey Holes have resulted in different answers by different authors. The

56 Aubrey Holes were more accurately placed radially than circumferentially: the circumferential deviation being as much as 21 inches. No circle inscribed on the ring of holes will touch every hole, however, when we attempt to superimpose a circle on them, something interesting happens. There are 33 holes that touch the line of the circle and all the holes on the north-east side are totally within the circle. This can best be shown by the diagram below.

Clearly the deviation from center was not due to error; it was planned by the builder. The result is that the Aubrey Center is slightly less than 3 feet from the Sarsen Center. This corresponds to the Contraction and Expansion Factors of the Great Pyramid which were 35.76277 Pyramid inches (35.8 British inches).

When Stonehenge is viewed as a chronometer, the Aubrey Circle functions as the date-line for the azimuths of the sun and moon as well as for all the bluestone alignments, telling the history of man. There are 44 such date-event indicators. Were we to move the Aubrey Circle in any direction these would all be negated, except perhaps one, if it were in line with the direction of the move. A 44 or 0 chance that these date indicators work (even if it were chance), is good authority for the correct position of the Aubrey Circle.

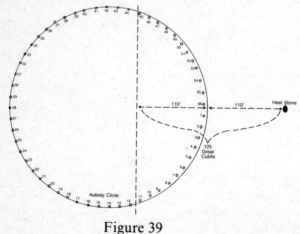

Figure 39

200

Appendix **III**

The
Axis

The problem of the axis has long been an item of confusion and dispute. Some British authors define it as a line passing through the middle of the intervals of uprights 55 and 56 of the Great Central Trilithon and uprights 1 and 30 of the Sarsen Circle. This would cause it to pass slightly to the north of the Heel Stone and coincide with the axis of the Avenue—a broad roadway bordered on either side by a bank and ditch. Other authors claim the true axis passes through the middle of the interval between uprights 15 and 16 of the Sarsen Circle. The Ordinance Survey Department seems to have assumed that an extension of the axis of the Avenue to the middle of the interval between uprights 1 and 30 was the logical axial line of the whole structure. By using this method the axis does not pass through the center of the monument, which is an obvious defect for an axis of symmetry. Wm. Flinders Petrie apparently ignored the Avenue and showed the axis as passing through the center of the monument. Fernand Niel* suggested that it was a mistake to assume that the axis of the Avenue is a prolongation of the axis of the monument. Gerald S. Hawkins† suggested that the main axis should follow the alignment of summer solstice sunrise through the center. R. J. C. Atkinson‡ also suggested that the axis points to the summer solstice sunrise.

---

*Fernand Niel, The Mysteries of Stonehenge, Avon Books, 1975, p. 133.

†Gerald S. Hawkins, Stonehenge Decoded, Dell Publications, 1965, p. 136.

‡R. J. C. Atkinson, Stonehenge and Avebury, Her Majesty's Stationery Office, London, 1959, p. 27.

STONEHENGE...A CLOSER LOOK

One of the first tasks of the builders, after the ground had been leveled, would be to determine the axis, thus giving it its center and orientation. The obvious orientation is toward sunrise at the summer solstice. All that would be needed for this imaginary line would be two posts, or markers, one at which to stand and the other across which to observe sunrise. This line of sight does, in fact, exist at the monument, as shown below.

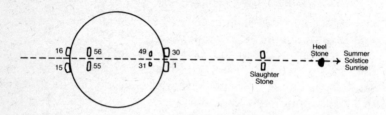

Figure 40

Using this sighting system at the time when Stonehenge was built, if the observer were to stand on the bank where this suggested axial line intersects its crest, he would see the full orb of the sun perfectly framed between the upright Slaughter Stone and its companion. (From this stance position, stone 67 of the Bluestone Horseshoe would not block the view, even though it stood on the axial line.) The interval between the Slaughter Stone and its companion was 3 feet and 15 inches which exactly corresponds to the apparent diameter of the sun as was seen from this position. Thus Stonehenge becomes the most precise solar observatory of the ancient world, making it possible to determine the summer solstice to within one day. A remarkable testimony to the knowledge of its builder.

However, if the axis followed the azimuth of the solstice sunrise, it would gradually change through the centuries because the sun slowly slips back along the ecliptic, causing its apparent position of rise to move gradually toward the east. The axis, therefore, probably followed the sunrise alignment at the time of construction, and whether it remains there or gradually moves with the sun is irrelevant.

Appendix **IV**

The Pyramid Angle

The azimuth of the summer solstice sunrise at Stonehenge has been given variously, by different authors, as:

49°34'
49°45'
49°47'
49°57'
50°26'
51°13'
51°18'
51°22'
51°30'
51°36'

The controversy goes grandly on! Why? Is not the relative position of the sun fixed? Yes and no.

In determining the azimuth of the sunrise at the summer solstice at Stonehenge there are a number of variables, all of which must be taken into consideration.

1. Because of the tilt of the earth's axis a phenomenon known as the precession of the equinoxes causes the sun to appear to slip back along the ecliptic. In about 26,000 years it slides backward one full revolution. Therefore, the azimuth of the solstice sunrise in 1973 B.C. would be to the left of its present position.
2. What do we consider as sunrise? Is it first flash, half disc, or full orb resting tangent to the horizon? From first flash to full orb requires about 4 minutes, during which time the sun moves nearly one degree to the right.
3. What is the altitude of the horizon? Is it the same today as when Stonehenge was built?

STONEHENGE...A CLOSER LOOK

4. Does the Heel Stone substitute for the horizon? If so, was it originally placed upright, or leaning at 30° from the perpendicular as it is today?
5. From what height should the sunrise be viewed? Should a six-foot man stand in the Sarsen Center, on the Altar Stone or on the bank behind the Great Central Trilithon?
6. Are refraction and parallax valid considerations? Both affect the apparent position of the sun.

Now that is a lot of variables! And they all must be taken into consideration—not one at a time but all together. The determining of the precise azimuth of sunrise when Stonehenge was built, therefore, appears impossible because of the quantity of unknown essential facts. But is it, in fact, impossible? Is there anything at Stonehenge that would mark it as a fixed position?

The Heel Stone has always been connected with the viewing of the summer sunrise. It was once called the Sunstone for this reason. The name Heel Stone probably comes from the Greek, *helios*, for sun.

A CBS Television Network program "Mystery of Stonehenge" filmed the solstice sunrise at Stonehenge in 1964. The photo shows a little less than half the sun's disc above the peak of the Heel Stone. The precession of the equinoxes has not separated the Heel Stone from the sun, for in 1973 B.C. it appeared on the horizon to the left, but its full orb appeared to be perched atop the Heel Stone. Through nearly 4,000 years the sun still crowns the Sunstone. This is shown by the illustration below.

The permanent position of the Heel Stone becomes a fixed marker for the azimuth of sunrise, unchangeable through time. The use of the Heel Stone for this all-important alignment eliminates all the variables, for the angle from north can be measured on the ground with no need of horizons. It matters not whether the builder placed the Heel Stone upright or tilted toward the center of the monument. Though the actual angle of sunrise-to-north has slowly changed

204

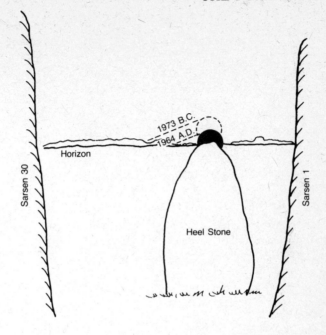

Figure 41

through time, its permanent marker has remained stationary. A line from the Sarsen Center to the center of the Heel Stone is 51°51′ from north, and it will never change.

Once again we stand in awe of the infinite knowledge and foresight of the builder! What man could have invented a device that would permanently fix the azimuth of sunrise? Yet the builder of Stonehenge did it with a rough unhewn stone!

This angle, 51°51′, is the famous Pyramid angle. It is often called the π angle because it gives to the height of the Great Pyramid the same relation to its square base as the radius of a circle bears to its circumference.

The angle that should permanently mark the sunrise on that remote plain in the British Isles was monumentalized in stone

205

167 years earlier by the angle of the Great Pyramid on the Gizeh Plateau in Egypt.

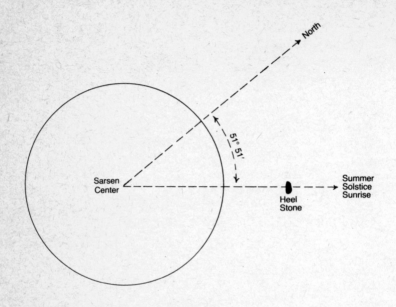

Figure 42

Appendix V

The Birth, Baptism and Death of Jesus

The date of Jesus' birth is generally accepted as 4 B.C. It may surprise some to find that no ancient historian, either ecclesiastical or secular, has recorded his birth as being in that year. Erroneous conclusions have been derived from certain statements of the Jewish historian, Josephus—conclusions which his records to not warrant.

Tertullian, one of the early Christian Fathers, born about 160 A.D., stated that Augustus began to rule 41 years before the birth of Jesus and died 15 years after that event. (Tert. adv. Judaeos c. 8) The date of Augustus' death is recorded as August 19, 14 A.D. This would place the birth of Jesus at 2 B.C. (One year is subtracted because there was no zero year between B.C. and A.D.)

In the same chapter, Tertullian stated that Jesus was born 28 years after the death of Cleopatra. Her death is recorded in history as occurring in 30 B.C.; again making the birth of Jesus to be in 2 B.C.

Irenaeus, who was born about a hundred years after Jesus, stated (iii. 25) that "Our Lord was born about the forty-first year of the reign of Augustus."Since Augustus began his rulership in the autumn of 43 B.C., it would place the birth of Jesus in the autumn of 2 B.C.

Eusebius (c. 264-340 A.D.), who was termed the Father of Church History, wrote, "It was the forty-second year of the reign of Augustus and the twenty-eighth from the subjection of Egypt on the death of Antony and Cleopatra" (Eccles. Hist.

i. 5). The 42nd year of Augustus began in the autumn of 2 B.C. and ended in the autumn of 1 B.C. The subjugation of Egypt and its incorporation into the Roman Empire occurred in the autumn of 30 B.C.; therefore the 28th year from that time extended from the autumn of 3 B.C. to the autumn of 2 B.C. Hence the only possible date for the birth of Jesus that would conform to both of these requirements would be the autumn of 2 B.C.

The common acceptance of the 4 B.C. date for the birth of Jesus is based on the oft-repeated statement that the death of Herod the Great was astronomically fixed by Josephus' record of an eclipse of the moon shortly before Herod died; and that eclipse has been shown to have occurred on March 13, 4 B.C.

Even simple reasoning would show the impossibility of the birth of Jesus being in that year, for the Biblical record not only shows his birth to be in the autumn, it shows additionally that considerable time elapsed between Jesus' birth and Herod's death, for the family fled to Egypt to escape Herod's edict that all boy babies should be killed.

The lunar eclipse on March 13, 4 B.C. was a small one (about 4 digits) and was visible in Israel from 2:00 a.m. until about 4:00 a.m. Coming at such an hour it would be noticed by very few people. Josephus was not a recorder of eclipses. In all his writings this is the only eclipse he ever mentioned. Lunar eclipses are common, often happening two or three times in a single year. It is hardly consistent, therefore, that Josephus would mention a small eclipse that happened in the early morning when everyone was asleep, and associate it with the burning of Matthias the day before. Speaking of the burning of Matthias by Herod, Josephus said "And on that very night there was an eclipse of the moon." To comply with the record of Josephus it is reasonable that we look for an eclipse of the moon that was noticeable by its magnitude, and occurred in the early part of the night when people were up to see it. The correct eclipse to which Josephus referred would have to comply with the following requirements:

  1) an eclipse not less than two months, but less than six months prior to a Passover,

2) be visible in the early part of the night at Jerusalem,

3) be of sufficient magnitude to be noticeable.

An eclipse that complies perfectly with these requirements occurred on the evening of December 29, 1 B.C., almost exactly three months before the Passover. It was an eclipse of about 7 digits, thus more than half the orb was obscured. The moon was already in eclipse when it rose over Jerusalem that night and continued for about two hours, so that even children would have been able to see it before being put to bed.

Since Herod died shortly after the burning of Matthias but two months before the Passover, his death would have occurred some time in January of 1 B.C. An ancient Jewish scroll, the *Magillath Ta'anith,* written during the lifetime of Jesus, gives the day and month of Herod's death as the 1st of Shebat. The 1st of Shebat in 1 B.C., by the Julian Calendar, would be January 14.

The world celebrates the birth of Jesus on December 25th—Christmas. The early Christian church did not celebrate his birth, thus the exact date was not preserved in tradition and festival observances. The first recorded mention of December 25 is in the calendar of Philocalus (354 A.D.) which showed Jesus' birth to be Friday, December 25, 1 A.D. The date is inconsistent with itself for December 25 of that year was, in fact, a Sunday.

The date of December 25 was officially proclaimed by the church fathers in 440 A.D., and was chosen because it Christianized the pagan festival of the Saturnalia. The winter solstice had meant the diminishing of the sun and its return again. Its central idea, the return of light, became the hope of the world in the birth of Jesus, the light of the world. The transition from paganism to Christianity was gradual, but became generally accepted after the fall of Rome in 476 A.D.

The exact date of Jesus' birth can, however, be determined from the available historical records. The information given in the Bible concerning the time of the conception of John the Baptist furnishes one method of calculation. Elizabeth, the mother of John, was a cousin of Mary and the wife of a priest named Zacharias. Luke 1:5 states that Zacharias was a priest of the course of Abia (Abijah). Verses 8-13 state that while Zacharias *"executed the priest's office before God in the order of his course"* he was given the message that Elizabeth would have a son and that they should name him John. In verses 23 and 24 it is recorded, *"And it came to pass that as soon as the days of his ministration were accomplished, he departed to his own house."*

The priests were divided into 24 classes (I Chronicles 24: 7-19) and each class officiated in the Temple for one week. The courses of the priests changed duty with the change of the week, *i.e.,* from the end of the Sabbath at sundown until the next Sabbath. Both the Talmud and the historian, Josephus, state that the Temple was destroyed by Titus on August 5, 70 A.D., and that the first course of priests had just taken office. The previous evening was the end of the Sabbath. The course of Abia (Abijah) was the 8th course, thus figuring backward we are able to determine that Zacharias ended his course and came off duty on July 13, 3 B.C., and returned home to Elizabeth. The conception of John occurred that weekend (13th-14th) and the birth of John would take place 280 days later, namely April 19th-20th of 2 B.C., precisely at the Passover of that year.

Elizabeth hid herself 5 months, and at the beginning of her 6th month the angel Gabriel appeared to Mary, telling her of Elizabeth's condition. At the same time Gabriel told Mary that she, too, would conceive and bear a son who would be called Jesus. Upon hearing this Mary went *"with haste"* from Nazareth to Ein Karim to visit Elizabeth, who was then in the first week of her 6th month. The time was the 4th week of December, 3 B.C. The 23rd of December of that year, according to the Julian Calendar then in use, was precisely the winter solstice. If this were the date of the conception of Jesus, 280 days later would place the date of his birth at September 29, 2 B.C., *i.e.,* 1st Tishri, the day of the Feast of Trumpets—the Jewish New Year. This day had been set aside in the Law of Moses as a holy day. How fitting that the holy Son of God should be born on that day!

The day on which Jesus was born was not only the first day

of the year but was also the first day of the 77th Sabbatic Cycle since the Jewish return from Babylonian captivity. From the re-establishment of the Sabbatic Cycles in Tishri 534 B.C. till the birth of Jesus in Tishri 2 B.C. was also a great Paschal Cycle of 532 years—a Paschal Cycle being the product of the *Metonic Cycle* (19) and the *Solar Cycle* (28), *i.e.,* 19 x 28 = 532 years.

Luke 3:1 clearly states that John the Baptist began his ministry in the 15th year of Tiberius Caesar. According to the Law of Moses a Jew was considered of age for the ministry at 30 (Numbers 4:3). Augustus had died on August 19, 14 A.D.; thus that year became the accession year of Tiberius, even though he had been involved in and associated with the Roman rulership before Augustus died. If John the Baptist had been born April 19th-20th, 2 B.C., his 30th birthday would be April 19-20, 29 A.D., or the 15th year of Tiberius. Thus the 2 B.C. date for the birth of John is comfirmed by the Biblical record. John was 5 months older than Jesus, making the birth of Jesus to be in the autumn of that year.

That his birth was in the autumn is further confirmed by the prophecy of Daniel (Daniel 9:24-27) which prophesied that there would be 3½ years from Jesus' anointing as the Messiah until his death. If his ministry began when he was 30 (Luke 3:23) and lasted 3½ years, and if he was crucified on the day of Passover (spring), simple arithmetic would show that his birth had to be in the autumn.

The Baptism

The ministry of John began when he was 30 years old in the 15th year of Tiberius, thus Jesus' baptism was also in the 15th of Tiberius, *i.e.,* 29 A.D. Luke 3:23 states that when Jesus was baptized he *"began to be about 30 years of age."* Why the indefinite term *"about?"* Would he not have been very careful to begin his ministry exactly on his 30th birthday? No! It was more important that he fulfill the antitypical significance of his ministry.

STONEHENGE...A CLOSER LOOK

The Atonement Day sacrifices of ancient Israel in the Tabernacle were types, or illustrations, of Jesus offering his body in sacrifice for the sins of the world. The Day of Atonement was the 10th day of Tishri. It was fitting therefore, to fulfill the picture, that Jesus offer himself on the Day of Atonement. His *"baptism into death"*—the offering of himself—was on the 10th of Tishri, 29 A.D., which, according to the Julian Calendar, was October 7th.

Did his water baptism, which was the outward or public symbol of his real death baptism, take place on the same day? On first thought it would seem natural to think that it did. Immediately following his water baptism the Biblical record states that he went into the wilderness for 40 days. Had he been baptized on the 10th of Tishri and gone into the wilderness for the next 40 days he would have broken the Law of Moses and sinned, for according to that Law (Deuteronomy 16:16) all Jewish men were required to appear at the Temple at Jerusalem during the days of the Feast of Tabernacles which began 15th Tishri. Assuming that he went to the Temple on the 15th, the whole of the next day would be required for walking to the Jordan. The day following began at sundown, thus the earliest possible day in which Jesus could be baptized and still fulfill all the requirements of the Law would be the 17th of Tishri (October 14, 29 A.D.).

His Death

It is from the prophecy of Daniel that we know the length of Jesus' ministry, *i.e.,* 3½ years. However, the same length of time can be deduced from the fact that he observed four Passovers during his ministry. (John 2:13; 5:1; 6:4; 13:1) He turned 30 in the autumn of 29 A.D. and the observance of four Passovers would reach to the spring of 33 A.D. But what was the exact day of his crucifixion?

From the Biblical record we know that the crucifixion took place on the day of Passover and that it was a Friday. The Passover was always observed on the 14th of Nisan, which in 33 A.D. was a Friday. According to the Mosaic Law the

Passover lambs were to be slain at 3:00 p.m. on Nisan 14. Josephus, who was an eye-witness to the killing of Passover lambs, stated (*Wars* VI, ix, 3) that they began to slay the lambs at the "ninth hour" (Jewish time corresponding to 3:00 p.m.). According to Mark 15:34-38 this was the precise hour that Jesus died on the cross. The Apostle Paul, some years later, explained that Jesus was the antitypical Passover lamb when he said, *"Christ our Passover is slain for us."* (I Corinthians 5:7).

The Passover lambs were always slain on the afternoon of full moon, *i.e.,* when the moon rose that evening it was full. This was because the first day of the month was determined by the observance of the new moon, and full moon always occurs 14 days later. On the afternoon of April 3, 33 A.D. the antitypical Passover Lamb died on a cross atop Golgotha's Hill outside Jerusalem. At 3:06 Greenwich time the moon eclipsed. When the moon rose over Jerusalem that night it was still eclipsed for 17 minutes.

Appendix **VI**

The
Great Cubit

The great cubit was given by God to the prophet Ezekiel in the year 573 B.C. It is described in Ezekiel 43:13, *"the cubit is a cubit and a hand breadth."*

Six of these cubits made one reed as described in Ezekiel 40:5 as *"a measuring reed of six great cubits long by the cubit and a hand breadth."* And again in Ezekiel 41:8 it is described as *"a full reed of six great cubits."*

Throughout the history of man several units known as *"cubits"* have been used, but this was a special one described as a *"cubit and a hand breadth."* The cubit to which the hand breadth is added is the ancient cubit known to the Babylonians as the moderate cubit, distinguishing it from the longer cubit then in use, known as the royal cubit. The moderate cubit was 18.14 inches and the hand breadth was 3.02 inches. When these two units are combined they give the beautiful and remarkable great cubit of 1.76 feet.

Our British mile, 5280 feet, which is in use today, is an even 3,000 great cubits. It has been demonstrated how the mile is commensurate with the other units of ancient metrology, thus the great cubit becomes part of that family. But just how ancient is the great cubit?

All of the Stonehenge Circles, with the exception of the Aubrey Circle, are evenly divisible by the great cubit. This gives the obvious evidence that the great cubit was known to the builder. Those marvelous ancient circles were, in fact, laid out on the basic unit of 1.76 feet.

215

STONEHENGE...A CLOSER LOOK

	Feet	Great Cubits	Reeds
Circumference of mean Sarsen Circle	316.8	180	30
Diameter of outer face of Sarsen Circle	105.6	60	10
Diameter of Bluestone Circle.	79.2	45	22½
Circumference of outer face of Inner Bank	1056	600	100
Each lintel.	10.56	6	1
Interval between Sarsen uprights . .	3.52	2	⅓
Long side of Station Stone rectangle	264	150	25
Diameter of Bluestone Horseshoe. .	39.6	22½	
Area of a square of same perimeter as mean of Sarsen Circle.	6272.64	2025	
Perimeter of a square drawn on Bluestone Horseshoe.	158.4	90	15
Perimeter of a square drawn on outer face of Sarsen Circle	422.4	240	40
Area of a square drawn on outer face of Sarsen Circle	11,151.36	3600	
Area of a square of same perimeter as outer face of Inner Bank	69,696	22,500	

The great cubit of 1.76 feet was monumentalized in stone by the lintels of that beautiful Sarsen Circle. The outer face of that perfect ring of lintels bears a radius of 17.6 yards. This unit of 1.76 is the basic unit of the circle. Each lintel is 6 x 1.76 or 10.56 feet which is the length of the reed given to Ezekiel in vision. One third of each lintel rested on an upright, one third spanned the gap and one third rested on the next upright. One third of each lintel is 3.52 feet or 2 great cubits.

The evidence is overwhelming! The great cubit was the basic unit used by the builder of Stonehenge. But how did the builder know this unit when it was not given to Ezekiel until 573 B.C.? God gave the great cubit to Ezekiel, therefore inductive reasoning leads to the probability that God was the Architect of Stonehenge. Inductive reasoning is not always accurate; so let's look further.

216

The great cubit is a unit which is commensurate with the geometry of the universe as shown below. The dimensions of the earth, sun and moon are evenly divisible by the great cubit, indicating that the Creator of these orbs used this unit.

	Miles	Feet	Creat Cubits
Diameter of sun	864,000	4,561,920,000	2,592,000,000
Diameter of earth	7,920	41,817,600	23,760,000
Diameter of moon ...	2,160	11,404,800	6,480,000

(The radius of the moon is 1080 miles and the diameter is 1080,000 reeds.)

The Creator who designed the universe used the same great cubit which Ezekiel saw in vision. The One who gave the vision of the New Jerusalem to John in 90 A.D. also used the great cubit, for the geometry of that prophetic city is evenly divisible by 1.76. Each side of the New Jerusalem is 7,920,000 feet which is 4,500,000 great cubits and the perimeter is 31,680,000 feet which is equal to 18,000,000 great cubits.

The mean circumference of the Sarsen Circle is 316.8 feet which is equal to 30 reeds. Thirty is a number associated with Jesus, as is 3168. The great cubit (1.76 feet) and its multiple, the reed (10.56 feet) bear the name of Jesus.

$2 \times 1.76 = 3.52$ ... The Way, $\eta\ o\delta os$, 352
$8 \times 1.76 = 14.08$ ... Saviour, $\sigma\omega\tau\eta\rho$, 1408
$13 \times 1.76 = 22.88$ ... Christ the Lord, $X\rho\iota\sigma\tau os\ \eta\ K\upsilon\rho\iota os$, 2288
$15 \times 1.76 = 26.4$ ... The Truth, $\eta\ \alpha\lambda\eta\theta\eta s$, 264
$3 \times 10.56 = 31.68$ .. Lord Jesus Christ, $K\upsilon\rho\iota os\ \text{'}I\eta\sigma o\upsilon s$
$X\rho\iota\sigma\tau os$, 3168

The relationship of the great cubit to Stonehenge is further shown by the list below:

1.76 feet = 1 great cubit
    17.6 yards—radius of outer face of Sarsen Circle
    .176 square miles—area of Bluestone Circle
    176 royal cubits—diameter of inner face of Inner Bank

2 x 1.76 = 3.52
   3.52 feet—average interval between Sarsen uprights
   352 yards—diameter of outer face of Sarsen Circle
   352 yards—circumference of outer face of Inner Bank
   352 = the way, η οδος

5 x 1.76 = 8.8
   88 yards—one side of a square of same perimeter as
      outer face of Inner Bank
   88 yards—long side of Station Stone rectangle

6 x 1.76 = 10.56
   10.56 feet—length of each lintel
   105.6 yards—circumference of mean Sarsen Circle
   105.6 feet—diameter of outer face of Sarsen Circle
   105.6 yards—perimeter of a square drawn on
      Bluestone Circle
   1056 feet—circumference of inner face of Inner Bank

7 x 1.76 = 12.32
   1232 square feet—area of Bluestone Horseshoe

8 x 1.76 = 14.08
   140.8 yards—perimeter of a square drawn on outer face
      of Sarsen Circle
   1408—Saviour, σωτηρ

9 x 1.76 = 15.84
   158.4 feet—perimeter of a square drawn on
      Bluestone Horseshoe

15 x 1.76 = 26.4
   26.4 yards—one side of a square of same perimeter as
      mean Sarsen Circle
   264 feet—one side of a square of same perimeter as
      outer face of Inner Bank
   264 feet—long side of Station Stone rectangle
   26.4 yards—diameter of Bluestone Circle
   264 = The Truth, η αληθης

18 x 1.76 = 31.68

    316.8 feet—circumference of mean Sarsen Circle

    316.8 feet—perimeter of a square drawn on
       Bluestone Circle

    316.8 yards—circumference of inner face of Inner Bank

    3168 inches—long side of Station Stone rectangle

    3168 inches—one side of a square of same perimeter as
       outer face of Inner Bank

    3168 = Lord Jesus Christ, $K\nu\rho\iota os$; $I\eta\sigma o\nu s$ $X\rho\iota\sigma\tau os$

45 x 1.76 = 79.2

    79.2 feet—diameter of Bluestone Circle

    79.2 feet—one side of a square of same perimeter as
       mean Sarsen Circle

    79.2 yards—one side of a square of same perimeter as
       inner face of Inner Bank

72 x 1.76 = 126.72

    1267.2 inches—diameter of outer face of Sarsen Circle

    12672 inches—circumference of outer face of Inner Bank

396 x 1.76 = 696.96

    696.96 square yards—area of a square of same perimeter
       as mean Sarsen Circle

    696.96 square yards—area of a square drawn on
       Bluestone Horseshoe

    69696 square feet—area of a square of same perimeter
       as outer face of Inner Bank

BIBLIOGRAPHY

Atkinson, R. J. C., *Stonehenge and Avebury,* London, Her Majesty's Stationery Office, 1959

Bergamini, David, *Mathematics,* New York, Life Science Library, Time, Inc., 1963

Bronowski, J., *The Ascent of Man,* Boston, Little, Brown & Company, 1973

Eban, Abba, *My People,* New York, Behrman House, Inc., and Random House, 1968

Edgar, Morton, *The Great Pyramid,* Glasgow, Bone & Hulley, 1924

Hawkins, Gerald S., *Beyond Stonehenge,* New York, Harper & Row, 1973

_____ *Splendor in the Sky,* New York, Harper & Brothers, 1961

_____ *Stonehenge Decoded,* New York, Dell Publishing Co., 1965

Journal for the History of Astronomy, Editor: M. A. Hoskins, New York, Neale Watson Academic Publications, Inc., June, 1974

Michell, John, *City of Revelation,* New York, Ballantine Books, 1972

Morris, Henry and John Whitcomb, *The Genesis Flood,* Grand Rapids, Baker Book House, 1961

Newall, R. S., *Stonehenge,* London, Her Majesty's Stationery Office, 1959

Newham, C. A., *The Astronomical Significance of Stonehenge,* Leeds, John Blackburn Limited, 1972

Niel, Fernand, *The Mysteries of Stonehenge,* New York, Avon Books, 1975

Patton, Donald W., *The Biblical Flood and the Ice Epoch,* Seattle, Pacific Meridian Publishing Co., 1966

Renfrew, Colin, *Before Civilization,* London, 1973

Russell, C. T., *Studies in the Scriptures,* E. Rutherford, N. J., Dawn Publications, 1916

Rutherford, Adam, *Pyramidology,* London, Institute of Pyramidology, 1970

Seiss, Joseph A., *Gospel in the Stars,* Grand Rapids, Kregel Publications, 1972

_____ *Miracle in Stone,* Philadelphia, Castle Press, 1877

The Standard Jewish Encyclopedia, New York, Doubleday & Co., 1966

Stone, E. H., *The Stones of Stonehenge,* London, R. Scott, 1924

Tompkins, Peter, *Secrets of the Great Pyramid,* New York, Harper & Row, 1971

Velikovsky, Immanuel, *World's in Collision,* New York, Dell Publishing Co., 1950

What is Stonehenge, Department of the Environment, London, Her Majesty's Stationery Office, 1972